MILLENNIUM

CLUES FOR THE CLUELESS

MILLENNIUM
CLUES FOR THE CLUELESS

CHRISTOPHER D. HUDSON
TIM BAKER
CAROL SMITH
RANDY SOUTHERN
LINDSAY M. VANKER

PROMISE
PRESS
An Imprint of Barbour Publishing

Developed and produced by the Livingstone Corporation.

Interior Design by Design Corps, Batavia, IL.

Cover Design by Robyn Martins.

Cover and Interior Artwork by Elwood Smith.

ISBN: 1-57748-566-1

Published by: Promise Press, an imprint of Barbour Publishing, Inc., P.O. Box 719
                   Uhrichsville, OH 44683.

Printed in the United States of America.

TABLE OF CONTENTS

SECTION 1
Y2K 1

SECTION 2
WHAT'S ALL THE HYPE? 27

SECTION 3
TECHNOLOGICAL TIE-UPS 53

SECTION 4
CHANGES 73

SECTION 8
YOUR PERSONAL FUTURE 171

SECTION 9
YOUR OWN SPIRITUAL HEALTH 213

SECTION 10
YOUR FAMILY AND THE MILLENNIUM 223

INDEX 231

•••

INTRODUCTION

What has been the most significant event of the last one thousand years?

• The invention of the printing press?
• Perhaps the American revolution?
• Maybe it was the industrial revolution?
• Or how about the invention of the computer?

That's a tough call, isn't it? There have been so many notable events, people, and inventions that it would be impossible to single out a *single* event.

What do you think the next thousand years will hold? What will a computer be able to do? How will travel be different? Will we live out the sci-fi fantasies we watch on Star Trek?

We face many unanswerable questions as we move from the twentieth century to the twenty-first century. Many of those questions are causing some people a great amount of fear. They fear the unknown and tremble at the thought of change. Many books, movies, and TV shows play off those fears and cause them to panic even more.

But never fear: This is NOT one of those books.

We're *not* going to tell you that the world will start skidding downhill on January 1, 2000. We're *not* going to tell you to build a bunker, buy guns and ammo, or seven years of groceries.

This book takes a more optimistic approach.

However, we are also *not* going to tell you that the best years of the world are ahead. We don't know that either. The world will probably be better in some ways, worse in others. The most important fact is that the world will be *different*. And THAT is what this book is all about.

Our society's culture, values, entertainment, business, and schools will continue changing so fast that you'll need to work hard to keep up. You'll need the information in this book (consider it an "Owner's Manual for the New Millennium") to help you be a twenty-first century Christian. You'll discover how you should prepare your church for the new millennium and share the gospel with people who don't know Jesus. You'll find ways to keep a level head and keep your spiritual health strong. You'll find all this in an interactive, fun, down-to-earth format.

More specifically, inside you'll find:

CATCH A CLUE

A Truckload of Clues. You'll learn tips about how to survive and enjoy the new millennium.

WIDE ANGLE

Perspective. Our emotions can run wild as we get caught up in millennium-fever. Sometimes we need to stop for a moment and look at the big picture. We'll help you take a step back.

WOW!

Amazing Stories and Facts. People have been looking forward to the new millennium since the last one! People have said some pretty funny things and told some unbelievable stories during the last thousand years. We've collected some of the best for you.

DON'T FORGET

Important Reminders. Certain things are important to remember as we become citizens of the twenty-first century. We've highlighted these for you.

THE BOTTOM LINE

The Bottom Line. We'll help you get beyond confusion by letting you know the most important stuff to remember.

THE BIBLE SAYS

Help from Above. We've highlighted a few key verses that will help you understand what the Bible has to say about the future.

The millennium is a time for hope, not for fear. We have a lot to look forward to as we watch God's plan unfold for our lives and for our world. As you face the future, you'll have questions. The good news, though, is that many of your questions are about to be answered. There's just one thing you need to do: *Read this book*. Feel free to read it *your* way: from cover to cover or skipping around to the parts that interest you most. No matter how you read it, you'll find it's jammed with good advice, great ideas, and entertaining thoughts. So turn the page and start reading. . . .

SECTION 1
Y2K

IS THE END OF THE WORLD NEAR?

THERE'S A LOT TO BE SCARED ABOUT

We face more uncertainties every day. As technology advances, our lack of control over the day-to-day details of life increases. When we think of the effects of a technological disaster such as the potential Y2K problem, we realize that our way of life is fragile at best.

Add to that potential natural disasters or international conflict and we can begin to see our world as a dark, futuristic movie with no Mad Max to save us from the bad guys. If we admit it, we aren't always even sure who the bad guys are.

There are a lot of factors that make us think the end of the world (as we know it) could be arriving right before our eyes.

The signs of the imminent return of Christ
As we watch the political fallout of the nation of Israel it becomes obvious that we are watching prophecy being fulfilled. As our world becomes connected through computer technology we see the stage being set for the potential rise of the Antichrist.

The alarms about the precarious health and longevity of the earth
Our planet has been warming for the last hundred years. While this is not the first time global warming has occurred, we are much more aware of

the reason it is happening now. We know about the hole in the ozone. We understand the ramifications of the pollution that we have sent billowing into our skies. We know there are consequences for how we have lived on the earth.

Technological crises such as the Y2K bug

We realize more than ever that our children's future will reflect more of the Jetsons' lifestyle than the Cleavers'.

Now we are suddenly faced with the precarious nature of a computer-driven existence.

Biotechnology and the moral confusion we sometimes feel about it

While we desperately want to learn how to heal wounded limbs and cure cancer, we are often unsettled by the research practices and the learning curve of biotechnology. Cloning leaves us unsettled. Research done with fetal tissue puts us on edge.

WOW!

Cloning

One thing you can be sure of: Whatever you hear about cloning is probably old news. There are so many conflicting rationales in regards to cloning of any kind, not to mention cloning of humans, that most research is done on the sly. Dolly the cloned sheep was not in the news until she was seven months old.

People are interested in cloning for a variety of reasons.
- They are curious.
- They want to recover someone who was loved and lost.
- They see it as a solution to infertility: Use your own cells to give birth to a baby who is the equivalent of your own twin.
- They see is as an attempt to improve the human race.
- It is a source of spare parts: bone marrow, body tissue, certain organs.

The cloning debate will go on for some time, but don't be deceived—the debates happen where we can't hear them. The research is being done far out of sight. By the time the debaters make their final point, it will probably be a moot one.

Warnings of an unstable economy

For years the naysayers have warned us that the investment world is not a stable world. They have cautioned us that our money seems safe, but it is, in fact, at great risk.

Now with the computer risks that the millennium poses the voices tell us even more loudly that a depression or financial bust is in store.

What if No One Cared?

"One third of the world will care significantly, one third will notice it, and one third will barely be aware of it."—historian Peter Stearns, on the advent of the third Christian millennium

Continuing threats of war and communism

We fear new enemies and different forms of war, and yet we are aware that terrorism has not vanished and unreasonable men in power are NOT a thing of the past.

THE THREATS TO LIFE AS WE KNOW IT

While the list above may represent our overall concerns about life today, there are some specific areas of danger that we face. Most of these areas are dangerous either because we don't know how to control the technology they involve or simply because we know the problem well but have no solution.

Chemicals

Whether you're talking about the chemicals we use to preserve our food, enhance our looks, or to keep bugs away from our groceries, the truth is we don't know fully what havoc those chemicals play in our world and in our bodies. There are so many new substances being created so quickly that we can't know what the long-term effects of them will be. We look around us and see the increased struggle with infertility, the increase of cancer of unknown origins, and have to wonder what price we are paying.

Overpopulation

Overpopulation is a giant that sleeps in the middle of the living room floor until we are all so used to it being there that we step over it without a second thought. But, the reality is that the livable space in this world is very small in light

CATCH A CLUE

BIO-1
Why Is Everyone Talking about Biotechnology?

Biotechnology is a group of scientific techniques that use living cells and molecules to make or modify products and to solve problems.

The idea of biotechnology (manipulating the natural world to make our lives easier) is not new. More than ten thousand years ago farmers bred plants and animals to get the best crops possible. Those same farmers used microbes such as bacteria and fungi to make cheese, wine, and yeast bread.

Some of our biotechnological advances in this century are:
- Viruses and bacteria used to make vaccines and antibiotics
- Microbial enzymes used to make detergents
- Bacteria used to treat sewage

of the speed at which our global population increases. This is not even taking into consideration the devastation that would be caused by a global weather event that would damage crops and leave us a warehouse away from starvation. We can't take care of all the people we have, yet between births and increased longevity of life our population is growing at both ends of the spectrum.

Biotechnology

The study of biotechnology touches our lives at every level. Stonewashed blue jeans, laundry detergents, human insulin, and home pregnancy tests are just a few of the products made with, or enhanced by, biotechnology. From genetic coding to the creation of enzymes, we are learning more and more about the biological ways to solve problems. The other side of that coin is that as we learn to manipulate the very building blocks that determine who we are, we become more responsible to use this knowledge wisely. We are also becoming more susceptible to having that very knowledge used against us. Cloning, gene splicing, fetal tissue testing, surgery in the

WIDE ANGLE

BIO-2
Genetic
Engineering

One of the main tools of bio-technology is genetic engineering, which rose to the surface of our understanding in the 1960s and 1970s. Until then, we knew how to manipulate whole organisms. But through a leap of technological progress geneticists are able to influence organisms at the cellular and molecular levels now. For example, instead of relying on the hit-and-miss techniques of crossbreeding to raise the perfect milk cow, genetic engineering allows scientists to insert a single gene—and the desirable trait it produces—without also transferring other genes and their potentially undesirable traits. It also allows the transfer of genes across species and genera. For example, an "antifreeze" gene from a cold-water flounder can be inserted into a strawberry plant to help strawberries grow in colder temperatures. Genetic engineering makes our life better in many ways, but you can imagine the horrific ways that this technology can be abused.

womb—all of these practices are a part of the biotechnological landscape of our day.

Germ warfare

Perhaps the most dangerous subset of biotechnology is germ warfare. Germ warfare is a prime example of the accomplishments of biotechnology used against humanity as a weapon rather than for humanity as a remedy. Whole regions can be contaminated without warning. Whole ethnic groups can sometimes be targeted. Testing facilities can become sitting ducks for terrorists who specialize in this

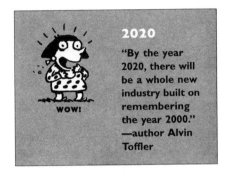

WOW!

2020

"By the year 2020, there will be a whole new industry built on remembering the year 2000."
—author Alvin Toffler

style of chemical battle. Thus far we have not found an effective way to supervise and limit these activities.

Terrorism

Besides guns, bombs, and ammo, terrorists also have access now to germ or biological warfare. Viruses are created rather than killed. Terrorists can innoculate themselves and then spray a few sprays of a lethal virus and wipe out a whole organization or even town. The virus can then disseminate before researchers arrive.

While the superpowers of our world seem to be laying down arms, the smaller armies are all too eager to pick them up. They are also less prone to moral inhibitions as they passionately represent their cause.

Nuclear threats

For the last decade the ultimate threat was the atomic bomb. At this point, almost anyone can make one. Plutonium, the most toxic chemical known to man, is now available in ways that we have never previously imagined. (Remember that a few ounces of plutonium was all that was necessary for the destruction of Hiroshima.)

While nuclear power is no longer a novelty, we have yet to put in place the proper controls for how, when, and where it is developed. This is an issue we will HAVE to confront in the near future.

WHY LIFE MIGHT GO ON ANOTHER THOUSAND YEARS

Even though we face high-tech crises of many kinds, there really are reasons to believe that there are good days ahead.

At one time at Walt Disney World General Electric sponsored an exhibit. The theme for the exhibit was "Now is the best time of our lives." The audience sat in a darkened auditorium and watched a stage turn like a lazy Susan. With each turn of the stage the audience would see a past stage of technological development in an American home—beginning before electricity was a component of every household. As electricity enabled more and more conveniences, the appliances on the stage were upgraded and the family became more modern. Only one thing stayed the same. At the end of each scenario a member of the family would say something like, "It will never get any better than this. Now is the best time of our lives."

This phrase became more humorous as the exhibit continued, because the audience members knew that life would get still easier and more convenient even though the plastic-and-wire family could never imagine how.

People living in times of earlier technology have been unable to imagine how things could get better. That is not the case so much today. In fact, we are so open in our thinking that the technological advances can sometimes overwhelm us with fear of the unforeseen by-products of our modernization. But while there is a downside to the pace of our culture and its inventiveness, there is also a bright hope.

Technology is not going to take us to a utopian global paradise. We know that from the Scriptures. We know that from observing human nature. What we don't know, though, is exactly where we are on God's timetable. Some of us THINK we know. But God's ways are higher than ours. No matter how bad or good we think things are they could get better or worse.

There are definitely some wild cards that we will face in the next millennium and even the next century. We can't control weather and natural disasters. We can't predict out-of-control men in control of nuclear weapons. But neither can we focus on these wild cards to the exclusion of everything else.

So let's play what-if. What if the world goes on another thousand years? What can we expect?

1. There will be an increased acceptance of other cultures.

This does not mean we won't honor cultural diversity, but it is one more step away from the prejudice and discrimination of the past.

2. We will have a less hostile military environment.
This is the first time in history that no major world power has war as an agenda item. That doesn't mean that wars will cease. But even now it is clear that the major national powers are not as likely to go to war.

3. Education will be even more prevalent and prioritized.

4. Better forms of global communication will be established.
This will then give a greater sense of global community. Personal

satellite antennas will enable people to be in touch more quickly and cheaply than ever before.

5. **Computers will continue to distribute power rather than centralize it.** While we are facing a major computer-related glitch at this point, it doesn't change the fact that computers have made information more available to the general public. While computers are responsible in part for increasing the momentum of our culture, they are also giving us more control of our schedules by allowing us to shop and learn from home.

Can You Watch Too Closely for Christ's Return?

THE BIBLE SAYS "Concerning the coming of our Lord Jesus Christ and our being gathered to him, we ask you, brothers, not to become easily unsettled or alarmed by some prophecy, report or letter supposed to have come from us, saying that the day of the Lord has already come. Don't let anyone deceive you in any way, for that day will not come until the rebellion occurs and the man of lawlessness is revealed, the man doomed to destruction. He will oppose and will exalt himself over everything that is called God or is worshiped, so that he sets himself up in God's temple, proclaiming himself to be God." (2 Thessalonians 2:1-4)

Since Jesus' death and resurrection, His followers have felt his return was imminent. If history has shown us anything, it is that life is unpredictable and just when we think we have it all figured out, it changes. The Bible teaches us to be prepared and watchful for Christ's return, but the Bible also teaches that He will come suddenly and unexpectantly. Playing the guessing game is fruitless.

Watching for Christ's return to the exclusion of living our lives abundantly is also fruitless. Part of the reason that Paul wrote the letter we now know as 2 Thessalonians is because some members of the church of Thessalonica had quit their jobs and were hanging around getting into trouble. Paul told them to go back to work and be about the business of Jesus' work.

"Now" will not be the best time of our lives if you consider our lives eternally, but that doesn't mean we can't celebrate the good things that humanity has accomplished.

ARE THERE ANY THEOLOGICAL IMPLICATIONS FOR THE YEAR 2000?

God's commands do not change with the year 2000. Neither does His very nature. What changes is the world around us. Facing this crisis will teach us more about our interconnectedness on Earth. Dealing with the crisis will teach us more about our ability to cope. Getting through the crisis will teach us about our ability to work together and find solutions together. There is an opportunity here to face difficulty and come out of it stronger and more able to see God no matter what the circumstance.

While there are not theological implications specific to the year 2000, there are theological implications that will help us face the year 2000.

NO SURPRISE TO GOD

It's the human way that while we may have a problem for a long time, when we suddenly become aware of it, we think that God has just become aware of it as well. But the year 2000, with whatever it may bring our way, is not something God is scurrying around at the last minute to face.

We must remind ourselves that God is above us. His ways are higher than ours. His abilities far outreach the most technologically advanced computer, programmer, or manufacturer. His power is far greater than the mighty sun, the most powerful nuclear bomb, or the most insidious lethal germ.

> *Many are the plans in a man's heart, but it is the Lord's purpose that prevails.*

Proverbs 19:21

GOD WILL MEET US THERE

Even with the perils of our world, the last 150 years have been historically stable. It has become easy, particularly for those of us in the Western world, to associate God's goodness with easy circumstances.

We have become practiced at seeing His hand in provision and blessing. We face a different challenge now: seeing His hand in adversity and instability. God promises us His presence—not favorable circumstances.

He will meet us in the year 2000 no matter what we face.

> *Where can I go from your Spirit? Where can I flee from your presence?*
> *If I go up to the heavens, you are there; if I make my bed in the depths, you are there.*
> *If I rise on the wings of the dawn, if I settle on the far side of the sea,*
> *even there your hand will guide me, your right hand will hold me fast.*
> *If I say, "Surely the darkness will hide me and the light become night around me,"*

*even the darkness will not be dark to you; the night will shine
like the day, for darkness is as light to you.*

Psalm 139:7-12

FAITH IS NOT ABOUT LIFE BEING EASY

God calls us to the same faithfulness in good times and bad. Many of us
have not experienced trials at the level that the Y2K glitch and the possible
coming instability in our world may produce. Though we work hard at
keeping our faith true, there is no purifying power greater than adversity.
Faith in God will stand the test of hard times. Faith in anything else will
crumble.

*Consider it pure joy, my brothers, whenever you face trials of
many kinds, because you know that the testing of your faith
develops perseverance. Perseverance must finish its work so that
you may be mature and complete, not lacking anything.*

James 1:2-4

CARE FOR THIS WORLD

Some of the difficulties we will face in the days ahead will be born of our
own past irresponsibility in caring for the world God has given us. From
the beginning, God gave humans the chore of caring for the earth. As we
have made our lives more convenient, we have sometimes done it at the
expense of the blue marble on which we live. The issues ahead of us will
call us back to a sense of stewardship over our world.

So God created man in his own image, in the image of God he created him; male and female he created them. God blessed them and said to them, "Be fruitful and increase in number; fill the earth and subdue it. Rule over the fish of the sea and the birds of the air and over every living creature that moves on the ground."

Genesis 1:27–28

LOOK AHEAD

When we look to Christ's return we hold more loosely to this world. It is a wonderful thing to realize that our citizenship is not really here. At the same time, though, this world and this life are a gift to us. The people God brings across our paths are gifts as well. When we are so enthralled with

CATCH A CLUE

A Lesson from King David's Men

When David gathered his army around him he gathered men of skill. Some were officers, some were brave warriors, some were experienced soldiers. There were groups from many different tribes. Of the tribe Issachar it was said that they "understood the times and knew what Israel should do." (1 Chron-icles 12:32).

The men of Issachar were valuable to David's army because they understood the landscape of their day and how to respond to it.

We follow the example of those men when we understand the nature of our times—whether it's Y2K preparation or an awareness of ecological concerns. We are responsible to know the needs of our world and what should be done.

heaven that we don't care for the earth or the people who live here, we are not effectively applying God's vision for our lives.

We live by faith, not by sight. We are confident, I say, and would prefer to be away from the body and at home with the Lord. So we make it our goal to please him, whether we are at home in the body or away from it. For we must all appear before the judgment seat of Christ, that each one may receive what is due him for the things done while in the body, whether good or bad.

2 Corinthians 5:7–10

SHOULD WE FEAR THE FUTURE?

There are many things are daunting us about the world around us and our future in it. Whether we are only looking as far as the year 2000 or whether we are looking ahead to the state of the world prior to Christ's return, or even whether we consider them both the same—we can feel fearful. Why?

There are a number of reasons; here are a few:

- Because change of any kind (even the best kind) produces anxiety in most of us.
- Because when we think about the world as we know it changing, we feel unsure of our readiness to face it.
- Because the future, by its very nature, leaves us out of control. We don't know what we'll face or how well we will face it.
- Because while we long for God to set the world right, this world is all we know. We're well-acquainted with it and have come to love and enjoy it. We don't know how heaven will be and so we fear giving up what we know.
- Because we have never experienced change at the global level like we will see it in the next thirty years. We know there will be difficulties and we dread them.
- Because with all the unknowns, we wonder how many more unknowns there will be that we haven't even thought or dreamed about yet.

Whenever Christians have a discussion about fear, 2 Timothy 1:7 comes into the conversation sooner or later.

> *For God did not give us a spirit of timidity, but a spirit of power, of love and of self-discipline.*
>
> 2 Timothy 1:7

This verse reminds us that fear is not something God sends our way. Because of this we know we can look to Him for power, love, and self-discipline rather than anxiety, worry, and distress. When we know that our fear is not from God, we do not have to yield to it or see it as permanent. When we look to

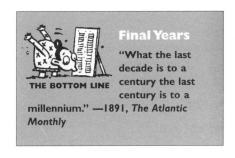

THE BOTTOM LINE

Final Years

"What the last decade is to a century the last century is to a millennium." —1891, *The Atlantic Monthly*

the future we may feel fearful, but it should just be a "stopping-off" place rather than a stage in which we live.

One of the greatest weapons against our fear of the future is the Word of God. Learn what God has to say about His provision for us now as well as in the future. Those promises, like the ones below, will not change no matter what we face whether it is biotechnological, macroindustrial, or just plain hard times.

> *But I will sing of your strength, in the morning I will sing of your love; for you are my fortress, my refuge in times of trouble.*
>
> Psalm 59:16

*But I trust in you, O
LORD; I say, "You are
my God." My times
are in your hands;
deliver me from my
enemies and from
those who pursue
me. Let your face
shine on your
servant; save me in
your unfailing love.*

Psalm 31:14-16

THE BIBLE SAYS

A Proverb about Preparation

In thinking about the Y2K bug and the potential end of the world as we know it, remember to keep a balanced view. Search for God so He can increase your wisdom.

"A prudent man sees danger and takes refuge, but the simple keep going and suffer for it."
(Proverbs 22:3)

And the other side of the proverbial coin...

"The wisdom of the prudent is to give thought to their ways, but the folly of fools is deception."
(Proverbs 14:8)

WHAT IF THIS REALLY IS THE END OF THE WORLD?

Now, brothers, about times and dates we do not need to write to you, for you know very well that the day of the Lord will come like a thief in the night. While people are saying, "Peace and safety," destruction will come on them suddenly, as labor pains on a pregnant woman, and they will not escape.

1 Thessalonians 5:1–3

WOW!

Will it Be So Bad?

Syndicated columnist Dave Barry on the Y2K bug: "Experts tell us that if it not fixed, when the year 2000 arrives, our telephone system will be unreliable, our financial records will be inaccurate, our government will be paralyzed and airline flights will be canceled without warning. In other words, things will be pretty much as they are now."

We know from God's Word that the world will not continue to improve, and we will never rid ourselves of all poverty, hunger, war, and strife. Maybe we could accomplish all this if we were not prone to sin, but the fact is that our natures *are* predisposed to sin.

And so as we populate this globe our sin destroys us—sometimes bit by bit and sometimes nation by nation.

We also know from God's Word that one day this world, as we know it, will end. While that thought might stress us out, it is reality. Chances are the circumstances in our world will get much worse before that time, but we can't really know how bad "bad" will be.

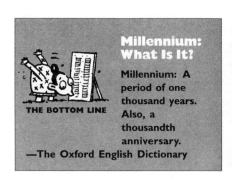

Millennium: What Is It?

Millennium: A period of one thousand years. Also, a thousandth anniversary.

THE BOTTOM LINE

—The Oxford English Dictionary

When Paul wrote 2 Timothy he was facing the end of life as he knew it. He was in prison on what we would call "death row." He wrote to his protégé:

> *Only Luke is with me. Get Mark and bring him with you, because he is helpful to me in my ministry.... When you come, bring the cloak that I left with Carpus at Troas, and my scrolls, especially the parchments.*
>
> 2 Timothy 4:11, 13

As Paul faced the end of *his* world he asked for the people he loved, the provision he needed, and the parchments (as much of the Bible as was written) he could learn and be comforted from. We can follow his example.

THE PEOPLE WE LOVE

Examine your relationships. Resolve conflicts. Say the things you need to say. Ask for the help that you need to receive.

THE PROVISION WE NEED

If we are about to experience "the beginning of the end" then we should prepare. We should be wise. Evaluate your life and your lifestyle. Simplify so that as our society erodes you can provide for yourself and the ones you love, and perhaps even minister to the ones less prepared than you.

THE PARCHMENTS (THE WORD OF GOD)

Read your Bible. If you do, you'll see that in truth, this world will not end without some definite warning signs. We read about them throughout the Scriptures. We see them happening around us in the world. We see them

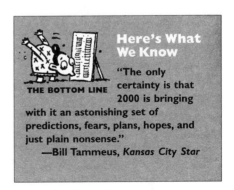

THE BOTTOM LINE

Here's What We Know

"The only certainty is that 2000 is bringing with it an astonishing set of predictions, fears, plans, hopes, and just plain nonsense."
—Bill Tammeus, *Kansas City Star*

reported in the news. Those signs tell us that this world will end in a sequence of events. Those signs tell us that no one can know for sure when that end will come.

The Word of God also tells us, not only to keep the end of the world in sight, but to prepare our hearts for the home-stretch. We were created to enjoy and glorify God. While we are still in this world, the more we connect with God and feel at home in His presence, the more we are prepared for the life after this one.

If we are indeed facing the end of the world and all the uncer-tainty that will bring, there is one thing we can be sure of: While everything feels out of control to us, everything is actually in God's control.

DON'T FORGET

Say What?

English:
millennium

French:
millenaire

Italian:
millennio

Spanish:
milenio

Czech:
tisicileti

Esperanto:
miljaro

> "Praise be to the name of God for ever and ever; wisdom and
>   power are his.
> He changes times and seasons; he sets up kings and deposes
>   them.
> He gives wisdom to the wise and knowledge to the
>   discerning.

*He reveals deep and hidden things; he knows what lies in
darkness, and light dwells with him."*

Daniel 2:20–22

We are in God's hand and He has a plan for carrying us home. On the way
we will face hardships and adversity. On the way we will experience
change and the stress that accompanies it. God gave no guarantees about
the journey, except that we would arrive safely at the end of it. That is the
promise that will see us through it all.

SECTION 2
WHAT'S ALL THE HYPE?

WHAT'S ALL THE HYPE?

Y2K: WHAT IS IT?

The Problem in a Nutshell

The Y2K or Millennium Bug is actually not any kind of bug at all. It's not an insect with six legs and an antennae.

It's not a computer virus sent through an E-mail with a deceptive subject line that will turn your computer's hard drive to jelly.

It's not something you catch.

It's not something you take medicine for.

But there is one other important thing that it is NOT...it's not something you can ignore.

The Y2K Bug is actually just a simple glitch in planning—a testament to the shortsighted quirk of human nature. It is as simple as the decision made by the early computer creators to use the last two digits of the year when they were typing in dates. "63" meant "1963." "81" meant "1981." That doesn't mean you only saw two numbers on the screen, but the computer stored all four. The computer only "thought" in terms of two-digit years. At that time this move saved them computer memory, which was a premium cost.

The creators as well as the programmers knew all along that there was a problem and that *eventually* something would need to be done about it. In fact, there have been warnings about it for thirty years. It's just that living in the urgency of the present tends to drown out the future. The year 2000 seemed far away in 1965, and in 1973, and in 1987, and even in 1996.

So the bottom line of the glitch is that in some computers, there are still just those two digits in the date. When the clock turns 'round to midnight on December 31, 1999 and it's suddenly the year 2000, how will those computers interpret that data? Will "00" mean "2000"? Or will they assume we've gone backwards 100 years? Will "00" mean "1900"?

This misunderstanding will affect any software that uses dates or time periods to keep track of information. It could also affect the very mechanism of the computer since computers contain chips that track time even when the machine is turned off. That is why some alarmists fear the whole computer world will just shut down.

WOW!

A Proverb, Then and Now

For the want of a nail, the shoe was lost;
For want of the shoe, the horse was lost;
For want of the horse, the general was lost;
For want of a general, the battle was lost;
For want of a battle, the kingdom was lost;
And all from the want of a nail.

For the want of 2 digits a date was lost;
For the want of that date, the year was lost;
For the want of the year, the software was lost;
For the want of that software, the info was lost;
For the want of the info, the business was lost;
And all from the want of 2 digits?

In your own computer this could affect calendaring programs, accounting programs, and spreadsheet programs, to name a few. On a larger scale it could affect whole industries. Large companies use computers for most tasks and certainly for tasks that involve scheduling. The Y2K glitch could, and probably will, affect the automation organizations such as

- Air traffic controllers
- Airlines
- Banking institutions
- Bus lines
- CPA firms
- Credit card companies
- Food distributors
- Hospitals
- Internal Revenue Service and its branches
- Long-distance telephone companies
- Nuclear power plants
- Paid parking companies
- Phone companies
- Social Security Administration
- Travel agencies
- Trucking and shipping companies
- U.S. Postal Service
- Utility companies

IT'S ALL ABOUT CONNECTIONS

To complicate matters, our current global culture makes this glitch particularly dangerous. Computer use has made us an interconnected world.

Electric companies are connected throughout states and regions and sometimes even further. Other industries are the same. While one division or area might have their software and hardware Y2K compliant, how will it be affected by the areas that do not? While one nation might be in good shape to face the turn of the century, how will it be affected by the nations that are not?

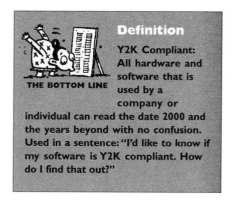

THE BOTTOM LINE

Definition

Y2K Compliant: All hardware and software that is used by a company or individual can read the date 2000 and the years beyond with no confusion. Used in a sentence: "I'd like to know if my software is Y2K compliant. How do I find that out?"

Interconnectedness doesn't merely affect members of the same industry. There are also chains within industry, in general, that are so interdependent that each link makes or breaks the chain. Let's say the factory that manufactures a national line of breakfast cereals has worked hard to become compliant in every way. That's great. But what if the trucking company they use to deliver the goods doesn't get their act together? What if the growers of the ingredients fall behind? What if the large store chains to which they sell don't function properly in terms of orders placed?

Because of this, it's not enough to know that you've taken care of your own computer. For better or worse, this is a community problem. In some cases that means a *worldwide* community problem.

Ultimately, we can't know exactly what will happen when the clock strikes midnight on 1/1/2000. Will operations cease? That is the question we don't *exactly* know the answer to. That is the Millennium Bug.

SOME CATEGORIES IN A NUTSHELL

The Y2K Bug or glitch will happen at several different levels of computer use: mainframes, PCs, and embedded chips. These different levels will affect your life in different ways.

MAINFRAMES

Mainframes are the large computers used by major corporations, utility companies, the government, and any other large agencies with thousands, or even millions, of pieces of information to keep track of. Mainframes were the first corporate computers. They were all we had before PCs. They filled whole rooms. They were the ultimate "server."

One of the problems particular to mainframes is that they are often older machines and the software they run is often older. Because they are older they are even more susceptible to year 2000 glitches.

To fix the problem in a mainframe you have to sort through lines upon lines of computer code. You have to find each and every place where a date is used, referred to, or depended upon. To put that into measurable terms, AT&T reportedly has 500 million lines of code. Many government organizations have more than that. That's a lot of sorting and finding.

You'll be affected by mainframes because of the huge agencies you depend on for utilities and government services. The good news is, these kinds of companies have probably been working longer and harder than anyone to be ready for the year 2000. The bad news is, if they aren't ready they will affect a lot of our society.

PC

There are literally hundreds of millions of personal or desktop computers operating today in both businesses and homes. They use a variety of software and are built by a variety of manufacturers. They are often used for a long time. They are often upgraded at different times and different levels and their software is mixed and matched.

In case you don't know much more about your computer than the color of its shell, a PC is a Personal Computer. The term PC is usually used for IBM compatibles, rather than Macs (Macintosh) or Apple computers. The truth is that since Macs were created later, they were created in a more Y2K compliant way than were PCs or IBM compatibles.

Evaluating the Y2K readiness of your PC happens on two levels: software (specific programs) and hardware (the actual machine with its processors and various boards).

In regards to software you have specific programs (like Quicken or Works) and you have your general operating environment (like Windows 3.1 or Windows 95). You'll need to check out both of these.

You might still have the same exact software that you had when you bought your computer. Perhaps you know the version of Windows and the version of Office. If you still have the same exact software then you probably know if your computer is old enough (1997 or before) to worry about it. If you don't know, you can probably call the place that you bought the computer from and ask them.

But if you've added, upgraded, or deleted software, you might need to work a little harder. Make a list of the software programs that you use. Usually when you open them they give you a version number. Write that down as well. If the version doesn't show when you boot (or start), look under the Help menu and see if there is a category that starts with "About..." When you click on it you'll probably get a dialog box that opens with a line identifying the program and the version. Write it down.

If you have the original documentation that came with your software, call the support line and ask them about the compliant status of your software. Call for each software program that you use as well as your operating environment.

If you don't have the documentation, call directory assistance and get a number to call. Be patient if you get passed around a bit. If you are comfortable going

The Chip

What kinds of activities might embedded chips control?

WIDE ANGLE

Air traffic controls
Airplanes
Automobiles
Cellular phones
Clocks
Construction equipment
Electricity flow
Food distribution
Gas distribution
Heating and air conditioning
  equipment
Intensive care units
Medication dispensing units
Microwaves
Military communications
Missiles
Nuclear cores in nuclear plants
Oil distribution
Oil drills
Pacemakers
Radios
Remote-control toys and robotics
Satellites
Security systems
Televisions
VCRs
Water flow

on-line you can probably also go to the web site of your software manufacturer and check there.

There are fixes for your computer. Often you'll have to pay for the fix, even from your computer's hardware or software manufacturer, but you should be able to find a way to face the year 2000 without purchasing all new equipment.

At the hardware level you really need to check with the manufacturer of your brand of computer and here's why: In each of these computers is a BIOS chip, a Basic Input-Output System. This chip calculates time. If that chip in the computer was purchased before 1997, it may very easily mistake 2000 for 1900. If it does it will affect software on the machine that calculates time (spreadsheet programs, checkbook programs or any financial or calendaring software).

There is really not an easy way for you to know the date your computer's BIOS chip was manufactured. If you, for some reason, can't call the manufacturer, call a computer repair shop near you.

And speaking of computer chips, read on...

EMBEDDED CHIPS

Embedded chips are minicomputers. They contain tiny circuitry that works to improve product reliability and speed. Embedded chips represent the biggest challenge of any of these categories for several reasons:

1. They are EVERYWHERE.
2. They are not usually upgradable. Rather than "software" or "hardware," they are called "firmware." Their function is built into the circuitry. You

don't install something new into the chip; you just throw the chip out when it doesn't work.

3. They are often old, unrepairable, and sometimes unreachable.

In short, embedded chips were not meant to be replaced; that's why they were *embedded*. Whether you're dealing with a greeting card that plays music or a kitchen appliance or a power transformer or a child's toy, usually the embedded chips were put there for the life of that product.

Embedded chips hold the most mystery and, some say, the most danger in terms of the Y2K bug. There doesn't seem to be a definitive way to know which chips will be affected and which won't or how many will be replaced by New Year's Day. But we do know that companies that bought and installed these chips have information about the chips. We also know that thousands of

THE BOTTOM LINE

Money's the Cause and Solution

Why did the original programmers choose to use only two digits? For cost reasons. The original computers were soooooo expensive and their memory was sooooo limited, that any way to save memory was used. One of the ways was to drop those two digits. While the original programmers have received a lot of the blame for this problem, they often shift that responsibility to the original computer company owners. These are the people who pushed the programmers to keep costs down and sometimes sacrificed good choices, for quick fixes.

It's interesting to note that the same people who pushed the programmers to cut these corners are, in some cases, the same people who still sell the computers and the quick-fixes for the Y2K bug. That is not to say that the Y2K bug is a deliberate moneymaker, but it is an ironic twist. Money's also the solution.

identical chips were made for many purposes. It's not as if each one has to be tested individually.

THE SOLUTION IN A NUTSHELL

Truthfully, the solution to the Y2K glitch is not a complicated one. You just go in and fix the way that the computer reads dates. You give the year four digits rather than two digits. Computer memory is not an overly expensive commodity so the cost is not prohibitive. How hard can it be to solve a problem that is all about two digits?

On one hand, not that hard. It's not difficult to solve the problem in any single computer. On the other hand, what is difficult in a gargantuan fashion is to solve the problem in every computer all over the world.

Since the 60s (or should we clarify and say the *1960*s) when computers were born, they have become an integral part of our society. They are embedded in our appliances as well as sitting on most of our desks. Our utility companies run their schedules by computer. Our banks run our accounts by computer. Our computers are even run by smaller computer chips.

It is not an exaggeration to say that computers are everywhere.

So while the solution to the Y2K problem may be simple, the enormity of the amount of computers that need to be fixed makes the problem worse than ever.

A SILVER BULLET?

According to folklore, a silver bullet through the heart can kill a particular kind of monster. Is there a silver bullet for the Y2K beast?

When you hear someone talk about a silver bullet in terms of Y2K, what they are talking about is a computer program that will automatically search through your computer's hardware and software and find the places where the years are listed or understood as only two digits. The program, or bullet, will then correct those places and go on to search for more.

The importance of a bullet is a matter of speed. Some experts say that a human programmer

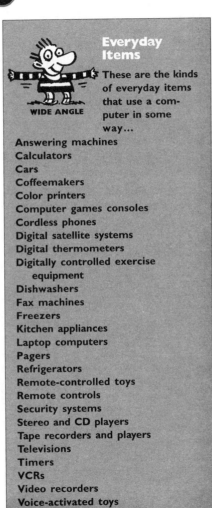

Everyday Items

WIDE ANGLE

These are the kinds of everyday items that use a computer in some way...

Answering machines
Calculators
Cars
Coffeemakers
Color printers
Computer games consoles
Cordless phones
Digital satellite systems
Digital thermometers
Digitally controlled exercise
    equipment
Dishwashers
Fax machines
Freezers
Kitchen appliances
Laptop computers
Pagers
Refrigerators
Remote-controlled toys
Remote controls
Security systems
Stereo and CD players
Tape recorders and players
Televisions
Timers
VCRs
Video recorders
Voice-activated toys
Washers and dryers

can correct about 100,000 lines of code in a year. For a company that has over five million lines of code, that means the company will need a lot of programmers and a lot of time. Some automated tools, or bullets, are reported to be able to correct four million lines of code per *hour*.

In the current literature by Y2K experts you can find as many opinions about the elusive silver bullet as you can find authors. One of the reasons for the differing opinions is the variety of computer languages. Not only are different software programs written in different computer languages, some individual programs are written in more than one language. To create a bullet that can shoot through every language in those programs is a daunting proposition.

WOW!

What's the Deal?

In truth it's not just the Y2K bug that is creating a panic. There are several other factors that leave people disconcerted as well.

1. A new millennium. Historically the turn of the century is a huge deal accompanied by alarmist's fancies and end of the world promises.
2. A leap year. Not only are we going to face the year 2000, but it's a leap year, an extra day. How will that affect the Y2K Bug?
3. Solar storms are headed our way as well, just before the turn of the century. These storms could disrupt our communication and electronic systems.
4. On May 5 of the year 2000 astronomers predict that the planets will align. Some say this could create every kind of disaster from earthquakes to killer microbes to even the dislodging of one or both of the polar ice caps.

Now, what were you worried about when the alarm went off this morning?

Nevertheless, while there may not be one silver bullet that kills the beast, as time goes by and problem-solving gains momentum there *are* automated tools being created that *are* quick and effective. Whether they will be effective enough to make us good to go when and if the embedded chip in the New Year's ball drops, we have yet to see.

WHY THE PANIC?

ISN'T IT OBVIOUS?!?!

Maybe it is and maybe it isn't. The truth is that most of us don't have the time or energy to research the problems and solutions of Y2K, or, for that matter, any other big issue that comes our way. That's what the experts are for, right? For most of us, just keeping our lives running is an overwhelming task. So we trust the experts to tell us what to worry about and what to do about things we worry about.

The experts that talk the loudest about Y2K are the experts that are the most concerned about it. Therefore, about all we hear from the experts are the problems we will be facing at the turn of the century. (The experts that are not worried about Y2K write books and articles about other things.) Not only do we hear about the problems, but most of us feel overwhelmed with them. When we give our typical line, "We don't have time to read about it, just tell us what to DO about it," the answers we receive are often so overwhelming that sometimes we'd rather not know.

TEST OUR COMPUTERS? Most people don't test their computers because they don't have time to deal with the fallout if the computers don't pass the test. Besides, we tell ourselves, by the time the real thing comes, everyone else will have it worked out.

STOCK UP ON FOOD AND WATER? Where? When? How? How much? Is it really necessary? Are we turning into backwoods alarmists who prepare for the end of the world every other week?

TAKE MONEY OUT OF THE BANK? That's fine if there's money IN the bank. But even if we have surplus in our accounts, we know that banks keep only a small proportion of money actually there and available to us. There wouldn't be enough money for us all to take ours out if we needed to. In fact, all of us running to take money out of the bank could create even more distress than the Y2K bug is supposed to create.

At the bottom of it, though, people panic because we are afraid of life spinning out of our control. On our worst day, we actually have it pretty good compared to our ancestors. To think about suddenly being catapulted back to an earlier technological age leaves most of us shivering with the sheer inconvenience of it.

We panic because the people we trust tell us to panic. We panic because we feel our way of life is threatened. We panic because we aren't sure there is anything we can do to fix this. We panic because we are afraid if there is something we can do to make this better we aren't sure we have the time. We panic because we don't feel sure that God will protect us from the worst-case scenario and, when it comes down to it, our human nature wants to trust in our own wits more than God's provision.

WHAT'S THE WORST-CASE SCENARIO?

So what is the worst-case scenario? It would go something like this…

At midnight, December 31, the electricity would go off, and it wouldn't come back on.

We would have no water after we used up what was in the pipes.

The parts of our world that have cold winters in December, January, and February and usually heat by electricity will begin to get very cold.

Because of the lack of electricity the world would be black around us

WIDE ANGLE

Top Ten Worst Reasons Why You Don't Have to Worry about the Y2K Bug

1. A crisis is good for organizations. It builds team spirit.
2. You've got lots of time.
3. It's a hardware problem and you do software.
4. It's not a problem….it's a "challenge"…no, it's an opportunity.
5. You think you'll just wait to see what happens before you react.
6. You believe that if you ignore the problem it'll go away.
7. You would enjoy the challenge of travelling backward 100 years or so technologically.
8. You can afford to be without your accounts receivable for an extended period.
9. You work better under pressure.
10. You believe this is all a plot by consultants to raise their hourly wage.

and throughout our cities.

Security alarms wouldn't work.

Phones could discontinue working.

Looters would take advantage of the situation.

The telephone lines would not work, so we would be unable to call the police.

If we went to the banks the next day (which would be January 1, a Saturday, and the banks would probably be closed) we would not be able to get cash out of the machine.

If we went to the bank on Monday we would still not be able to get money because the computers would be down.

The stock exchange would be nonfunctioning.

Hospitals, running on emergency generators if they had them, would be experiencing difficulty in regard to any form of automation, including IV medicine dispensers, monitors, and even imaging machines—not to mention record keeping and insurance information. (Imagine THAT emergency room!)

So, if you're looking for the worstcase, the most hysteria, the loudest alarm, the picture can be very dark. Reality, though, *is that the worst-case scenario is probably not going to happen*. While there will be some minor disruptions, every single system will not break down at one time. Preparing for the worst might seem like a good option, but you'll be spending a lot of energy battling demons that won't be there to meet you when the war ensues.

WHAT SHOULD YOU DO?

First of all, just look around your home. Evaluate what functions depend on electricity or automation.

Check your computers at home. Upgrade your software. If you're computer was purchased before 1997, take it to a computer repair shop and have them appraise its readiness for you.

Call manufacturers of your appliances that you believe contain embedded chips. Better yet, check the Internet. There is a variety of "Y2K compliant" lists for the manufacturers of household appliances and a host of other gadgets.

Evaluate your own place of business and how your job might be affected by this problem.

Sit down and make a list of the areas that make you feel vulnerable (your bank, any stocks and bonds). Contact those agencies or organizations. Most should have a standard response and even perhaps written information that will answer your questions in regard to their Y2K preparations.

Talk to the utility companies in your area and ask them if there are any precautions you should take.

Pay off every debt that you can.

Invest your money in something stable like government savings bonds or U.S. Treasury bills.

Secure paper records (hard copies) of your monthly bills and yearly investments, banking accounts, insurance records, and investments.

Make sure you know where your personal records are in case any need to be re-created:

Birth certificates

Passports

Property deeds

Tax records for the last five to seven years

Mortgage information

Medical records

No matter how little of an alarmist lives inside of you, keep in mind that Y2K is NOT a hoax. Even the mildest of scenarios describes a fallout at the level of a severe snowstorm or thunderstorm. So how would you prepare for that?

- Some extra staples
- Some extra water
- Gas for the generator if you have one
- Candles or oil lamps and matches
- Flashlights
- Wood for the fireplace
- Oil or battery-fueled heaters

MYTHS AND URBAN LEGENDS

MYTH AND LEGEND #1

There's no Y2K ANYTHING. It's all a hoax some geeks made up so they could make money off the panic. Forget about it.

Well…

It is true that some people are going to make some money off of the Y2K panic. It's also true that some people will make money from the information that they share about the Y2K glitch and how to prepare for it. But the basis of the problem, the two digit years in the dates and the confusion they might cause—that is real. It is NOT a hoax. No one made it up, in fact, it's been a point of discussion for thirty years. It's just that human nature being what it is, the future seems so far away until it's right here upon us.

MYTH AND LEGEND #2

The total cost of repairs could be more than $600 billion.

That's more than the 1996 gross national products for the whole nation of Canada, for crying out loud! Fixing this glitch is definitely going to cost time, money, and resources, but this estimate is a little high. Maybe this myth originated when one of the original Y2K experts estimated that fixing the date problem would cost about $1 per line of code. At that rate, you might reach half of the $600 billion mark, but not quite that high. Just how many groceries could you buy for $600 billion anyway?

MYTH AND LEGEND #3

All the airplanes will fall out of the sky at 12:01 A.M. 1/1/2000.

There are concerns about the programs used by air traffic controllers and the scheduling software used by airlines and airports. But there is legitimate testing going on even as you read this. Many airlines and airports are passing with flying colors.

MYTH AND LEGEND #4

This problem will only occur on January 1, 2000.

Actually, no. In some cases it is already occurring. Think about programs that need to forecast data, for instance, credit cards that expire after January 1, 2000. If the computer reads that as 1900, the card is already expired. There are some documented cases of this kind of problem already. What about quarterly forecasts? They will run into the year 2000 when they start their fourth quarter. This problem, like most other problems, will be a process to work through. In your own PC the clock turning to 2000 might kick off a response, but worldwide it will be a more drawn-out procedure.

MYTH AND LEGEND #5

If my computer is relatively new, I won't have a problem.

You know what? It's worth checking. How long did your computer sit on the shelf before you bought it? More importantly, how old are your programs?

CATCH A CLUE

Red Cross Y2K Survival Checklist

If anyone knows how to prepare for a crisis, it's the Red Cross. They've faced about every crisis that has come humanity's way. The following suggestions are included in the Red Cross list for Y2K preparation.

- Check with manufacturers of any essential computer-controlled electronic equipment in your home to see if that equipment may be affected (for instance, fire and security alarm systems, programmable thermostats, appliances, consumer electronics, garage door openers, electronic locks).
- Stock enough supplies to last several days to a week for yourself and those who live with you (for instance, nonperishable foods, stored water, and an ample supply of prescription and nonprescription medications that you regularly use).
- As you would in preparation for a storm of any kind, have some extra cash or travelers' checks on hand in case electronic transactions involving ATM cards, credit cards, and the like cannot be processed. If you withdraw money from your bank, do it in small amounts well in advance of 12/31/99.
- Keep your automobile gas tank above half full.
- Make a safe plan to keep warm.
- Have plenty of flashlights and extra batteries on hand.
- Examine your smoke alarms now. If you have smoke alarms that are hard-wired into your home's electrical system (most newer ones are), check to see if they have battery backups.
- Have a battery-operated radio available to hear any reports if there is a power outage.

MYTH AND LEGEND #6

We'll have a worldwide blackout.

Actually, there might be some problems with electricity, but utility companies rank right up there in the top five for preparation along with telecommunications companies and the banking industry.

MYTH AND LEGEND #7

There is an embedded chip on every power pole along your street and in your city. We'll never get them all tested!

No, there's not. There may be embedded chips in the transformers that are in the power station, but not on the poles. And if they were there, you wouldn't test them on the pole. You'd go back to the schematics of those thousands of identical chips and check there. Don't—we repeat—DON'T go climbing any power poles.

SECTION 3
TECHNOLOGICAL TIE-UPS

TECHNOLOGICAL TIE-UPS

WHO NEEDS IT?

THE BOTTOM LINE

Upgrade or Upheaval?

"A new technology does not add or subtract something. It changes everything." —Neil Postman, author of *Technopoly*

It's surprising just how much we depend on modern technologies today. Try to imagine, for example, life without electricity. Besides what we've seen in history books, or experienced on wilderness adventures, a day-to-day life without electricity is hard to envision.

A Christian college near Chicago recently experienced such a life firsthand. Late one Monday night, several cables shorted-out, shutting off the school's electricity for the next twenty-four hours. What did this mean for the students? No alarm clocks, no coffee, and no hot showers. They couldn't listen to their stereos, watch TV, jog on a treadmill, play video games, or surf the Net. In fact, they couldn't even do homework unless they sat outside or drove off-campus because they had no working lights or computers and the library was closed.

The administration also faced similar problems. Fire alarms didn't work, cafeteria workers couldn't cook, and the school network had shut off. In addition, the academic buildings had no lights and professors couldn't use overhead or slide projectors. Even the clock tower stopped operating. College life was put on hold.

So, how would you react in such a crisis? This college burst with its newfound freedom. When the administration canceled classes for the day, students flooded outside to enjoy the 72-degree day. By eight o'clock in the morning, students had filled the tennis courts completely. Many opted to lay out in the sun, play the guitar, or study on the lawn while others played various outdoor games. Preppy students, environmentalists, musicians, athletes, and science majors joined in everything from duck-duck-goose,

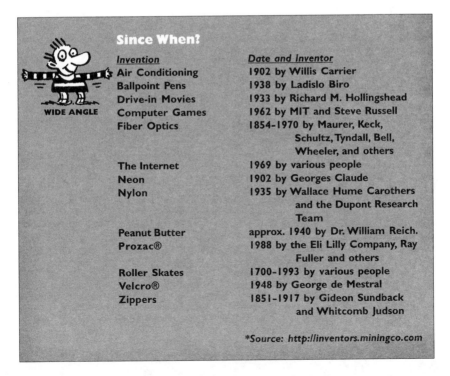

Since When?

WIDE ANGLE

Invention	*Date and Inventor*
Air Conditioning	1902 by Willis Carrier
Ballpoint Pens	1938 by Ladislo Biro
Drive-in Movies	1933 by Richard M. Hollingshead
Computer Games	1962 by MIT and Steve Russell
Fiber Optics	1854–1970 by Maurer, Keck, Schultz, Tyndall, Bell, Wheeler, and others
The Internet	1969 by various people
Neon	1902 by Georges Claude
Nylon	1935 by Wallace Hume Carothers and the Dupont Research Team
Peanut Butter	approx. 1940 by Dr. William Reich.
Prozac®	1988 by the Eli Lilly Company, Ray Fuller and others
Roller Skates	1700–1993 by various people
Velcro®	1948 by George de Mestral
Zippers	1851–1917 by Gideon Sundback and Whitcomb Judson

*Source: http://inventors.miningco.com

leapfrog, and steal-the-bacon to freeze tag, ultimate Frisbee, and soccer. The cafeteria staff lugged out grills for a huge picnic of chicken, corn, fruit, and lemonade. Even after dark, the festivities continued. A ska band performed on the porch of a campus house. Various students played ghost-in-the-graveyard or rotten-sardines outside. And many simply went to bed. But by 1:30 that morning, the electricity came back on and life returned to normal.

Just as this college saw on that unusual spring day, American life changes drastically without electricity. God has given us creative minds and many resources to help us survive and enjoy life even without the manmade technology we rely so heavily upon. See if you too can come up with alternatives for the ten modern technologies listed below:

1. Cars

_____

_____

_____

_____

2. Radios/CD players/Tape players

_____

_____

_____

_____

3. TVs/VCRs/Movies

_____

_____

4. Microwaves

5. Curling irons/Hair dryers

6. Video games

7. Typewriters/Word processors/PCs

8. Alarm clocks

_____

_____

_____

_____

9. Lamps

_____

_____

_____

_____

10. Telephones

_____

_____

_____

_____

Opinions

Our God-given creativity has allowed us to develop the many technologies we rely on today. But is technology actually good? Or is it evil? Does God approve of these human advances? Many people have debated these questions over the years. Nevertheless, they have reached some very different conclusions. As we tell you about these different opinions, try to ask yourself where you would fit in. Do you believe technology is good or evil? The next millennium will be filled with new technologies. How will you respond to them? Let's take a look at the different extremes.

First, on one extreme, are the technophobes. These people fear and oppose all forms of modern technology. In fact, they believe all technological advancement is evil. Technophobes prefer living the "old-fashioned way" and don't like any complicated devices. Instead, they avoid technology altogether and try to live only by natural resources. The Amish, for example, might fall into this category.

The next group, the Neo-Luddites, oppose many forms of technology, but not all. Like the Luddites of the 1800s, this group believes that overusing technology hurts personal relationships and the diversity of nature. As a result, the Neo-Luddites mainly object to technologies they believe will destroy jobs and the environment.

On the other hand, some support technology on a more moderate level. These "moderates," as we'll call them, appreciate the benefits of progress but try not to depend too heavily on technology. They are more skeptical than technophiles (who we'll discuss in a minute) about the good that technology can bring, but recognize that it does bring some good.

While moderates use many forms of technology, they make a conscious effort not to overuse or abuse it.

Finally, on the opposite extreme are the technophiles. This group is virtually obsessed with technology. They spend much of their time dabbling with new gadgets—especially with computers. Technophiles believe that technology can solve any problem eventually and advocate all kinds of advancement. In essence, these people are fanatics about technology and may be referred to as "techno-junkies" as well.

WOW!

Who Is Ned Lud?

General Ned Lud is the imaginary hero of the nineteenth-century Luddites. According to legend, Lud inspired many workers to protect their skills and jobs against England's mechanized looms. So, the Luddites sabotaged these looms and led swing riots throughout southern and western England. Nevertheless, the British government suppressed these rebels before the revolution could spread to France. But even though the original cause didn't succeed, the story lives on. Now, the term "Luddite" is applied to those afraid of technology, even if they're not using sabotage to protect their jobs.

So, now that you've read about these different approaches to technology, ask yourself again, "Where do I fit in?" Are you afraid that technology is sinful and will eventually destroy the world? Do you believe most, but not all, technologies are harmful to people and the environment? Or do you believe that technology's benefits outweigh its bad effects? Do you believe it is the solution to all our problems? Place on X on the line below to indicate your belief about technology:

Technophobe   Neo-Luddite   Moderate   Technophile

AND SCRIPTURE SAYS...

Does the Bible really say something about how we should view technology? Actually, it says much more than you might think. While the Bible might not speak directly to telephones, computers and genetic engineering, it does provide us with many solid principles that apply to these areas of life.

Not a Creative Bone in Your Body?

First, look at creation. Genesis 1:27 says, "God created man in His own image, in the image of God He created him; male and female" (NASB). What does it mean to be created in "the image of God"? What makes us different from the animals? Some believe that human imagination is part of what makes us like God. We don't act only on instinct but, like our Creator, we have the ability to create, plan, and imagine. For example, God gave

WOW!

Pros and Cons

Clocks—provided greater precision for science and business but also a more frantic, less relaxed atmosphere

Printing Press—made the Bible readily available to all but also floods us with trivial information

Cars—gave us faster and greater mobility but are also the number one killer in the United States today

Photographs—showed us the secret of how birds fly which helped us take off but also led to accessible, private pornography

Telephones—provided quicker communication for friends and businesses but forced irresistible interruptions on us

Radio—gave us instant access to worldwide news but also surrounded us with constant noise

Adam the job of naming animals in the Garden of Eden. Genesis 2:19 says, "And whatever the man called each living creature, that was its name." How could anyone come up with a name for zebras, duck-billed platypuses, or hippopotamuses without a little creativity?

So we can consider creativity a gift from God. He has given us the ability to imagine more efficient, enjoyable ways to live. With our God-given creativity and knowledge, we have created many beneficial technologies. Below, list several technologies you believe have improved modern living:

_____

_____

_____

_____

_____

_____

ON THE OTHER HAND

On the other hand, we can easily misuse this creativity. Several times, the Bible talks about people using their imagination for evil purposes. Romans 1:28–32 (NASB) calls such people "inventors of evil" who don't acknowledge God anymore. Because all humans are sinful, we all have the capacity to use our creativity against God and His plan. If such a mind isn't restrained by self-discipline and the Holy Spirit, the possibilities for evil are endless. Technology can be an outlet for evil as well as good. So, this time list several technologies you believe have been used to corrupt modern living:

_____

_____

_____

_____

_____

_____

_____

It's important to distinguish evil from technology. Technology in itself isn't evil. *People* use technology for evil things. For example, there are many sites on the Internet that are filled with evil, but that doesn't mean the Internet itself is evil. The internet has many good and noble uses. We should be careful not to write off a new technology because it has the potential for evil use (doesn't every technology?).

ANCIENT TECHNO-JUNKIES?!

Let's look at a specific example in the Bible of how technology can be used for good and for evil. Second Chronicles 26 records the story of King Uzziah, who began ruling Judah when he was only sixteen years old. Uzziah was a good king who sought to do God's will. As a result, the Lord gave him the capabilities through new warfare technologies to defeat many of Judah's enemies and fortify God's holy city. Verse 15 says, "In Jerusalem he made engines of war invented by skillful men to be on the towers and on the corners for the purpose of shooting arrows and great stones."

WOW!

Fun Fiscal Facts!

"1. In the past, people have used tobacco, dried fish, feathers, rum, and seashells as money.

2. The largest coins ever issued were copper Swedish plate money in 1644-1722. Each coin weighed about forty-five pounds.

3. In 1995, customers only used credit and debit cards for about 14 percent of their transaction totals. Now, credit card usage is increasing at a rate of 10 percent per year and debit card usage at a rate of 40 percent a year. Cash and check usage, however, is declining."
—Jack Weatherford, *The History of Money*

These inventions and new technologies helped Uzziah win battles for the

Lord and His people. "Hence his fame spread afar, for he was marvelously helped until he was strong" (NASB).

Soon, however, King Uzziah forgot the purpose of these battles. "But when he became strong, his heart was so proud that he acted corruptly, and he was unfaithful to the LORD his God" (26:16 NASB). Rather than using these new technologies for God's honor, Uzziah let his success harden his heart toward God. He felt he was so powerful, he could do anything he wanted! Wrong! When Uzziah began overstepping his role, God punished him. In fact, God took Uzziah's rebellion so seriously, that He struck him with the terrible skin disease of leprosy. In the end, Uzziah died a sinful, isolated, sickly king instead of the godly, innovative, successful king he once was.

We should learn from Uzziah's mistake. God has also provided us with many technologies to use for His glory. Just think how many timesaving devices we have that could free us up for serving God and others! We no longer need to wash our clothes by hand or iron every sheet and shirt. And consider how many technologies help us spread the gospel to great numbers of people. We have printing presses, microphones, radios, television, and swift mobility. But God has also provided us with many technologies for our own well-being. We have greater medical capabilities, photographs to capture visual memories, and telephones for quicker communication. Technology has definitely provided our society with many benefits.

Nevertheless, just as technology has great potential for good and for the glory of God, it has as great a potential for evil. Unlike Uzziah, we must not become so proud with our great capabilities that we forget about God. For example, just as medicine has helped infertile couples have children, we must remember that "Children are a gift of the LORD" (Psalm 127:3, NASB). Just as inventions such as the Internet provide us with greater access to valuable information, we must remember Paul's exhortation in Ephesians

5:15–16, "Therefore be careful how you walk, not as unwise men, but as wise, making the most of your time, because the days are evil" (NASB). Like food or sleep, technology can help us grow and can refresh us. But if we overuse or misuse the resources we're given, we can become spiritually and physically sick, fat, and lazy.

MODERN CHRISTIANS

So how should Christians approach technology? First, we must recognize that technology, like any other resource in life, has great potential for good and for evil. Therefore, we should use discernment as we exploit technology. For example, we should establish strong, God-honoring standards for viewing films, surfing the Internet, using the telephone, and we should be careful not to become obsessed with the newest gadgets.

In addition, we must take care to remember God in everyday life. This requires taking time out from the noise and busyness of our technological world to spend time with Him in prayer and in His Word. Here are some suggestions as to how you can do this:

- Wake up early in the morning, before radios are blaring and cars zooming down the street, to "be still" before God.
- Start a prayer list to help focus your mind on important issues and watch God work in people's lives. Choose a psalm to pray through each day.
- Journal about your spiritual journey to help you think through what you've been learning.
- Take an occasional retreat from technology and have a quiet day to thank God for His many gifts and to rest your heart and mind.
- Before bed, read a little from books that help you understand God or how to please Him.
- Sing praises to Him with your voice and with instruments instead of

always relying on Christian CDs or cassettes to prompt your heart to worship.

- Set aside Sunday as a day for church, worship, and rest from the craze of modern life.

Third, we must take time to notice God in nature. Romans 1:20 says, "For since the creation of the world His invisible attributes, His eternal power and divine nature, have been clearly seen, being understood through what has been made" (NASB). God's creation reveals much to us about His character.

WOW!

**True Religion...
or Trouble?**

Searching under "God" using the AltaVista search engine shows over five million web pages. In addition, the Yahoo engine covers 16,000 pages under its subheading "Faith and Practices." The religions listed there include Christianity, Judaism, and Islam as well as Animism, Satanism, and Voodoo.

Consider how many times David and Solomon used nature to illustrate God's power or goodness in the Psalms and Proverbs. It is important that we don't rely so heavily on manmade devices that we neglect to see God in the world outside. Take time to enjoy the outdoors and study God's nature in creation. How can you do this?

- Take a walk at sunrise before breakfast.
- Plant a garden or keep fresh flowers on the kitchen table.
- Set up a bird feeder outside your window.
- Climb a tree and read a book.

- Have a picnic in your backyard.
- Ride your bike or hike on paths in local woods.
- Take a trip to a national park.
- If you're real adventurous, go on a backpack or canoe trip where you'll be completely separated from telephones, TVs, and even showers for a few days.

Finally, we shouldn't neglect either work or rest. We live in a society that prioritizes entertainment and personal comfort. Largely due to the on-slaught of entertainment technology, both children and adults have trouble staying on task for long. In fact, many schools and churches have resorted to offering entertainment in order to capture the attention of our restless minds. We think, "If it's not fun, its not worth it."

Christians have the difficult job of applying the Bible verse that says we should prepare our minds for action and have a sober spirit (1 Peter 1:13 NASB). It's easy to give into lust for amusement. But instead, we should discipline ourselves to work hard. The good news is that such work brings a sense of satisfaction. Solomon says in Ecclesiastes 5:18, "Here is what I have seen to be good and fitting: to eat, to drink and enjoy oneself in all one's labor in which he toils under the sun during the few years of his life which God has given him; for this is his reward" (NASB).

On the other hand, we should be careful not be so tied to our comput-ers, cell phones, and vacuum cleaners that we forget to rest from our work as well. As God exemplified for us in Genesis 2, we should take a day to rest from our labor. In fact, resting gives us time to rejuvenate and work more efficiently so that we'll have more time to rest so that we can gain strength to work harder later so that. . . Whew! Just take a break once in a while. Your family and friends will thank you.

So, now that we've looked at the biblical view of technology and have considered some ways Christians should respond to modern progress, let's go back to the chart we looked at earlier. Where do you think Christians should fit on the line? Place an X on the line to indicate your belief about technology now.

Technophobe   Neo-Luddite   Moderate   Technophile

SECTION 4
CHANGES

CHANGES LIKE YOU'VE NEVER SEEN

TECHNO CHANGES

You might remember life without a microwave or remember trying to find something to do on Friday night when renting a video wasn't an option yet. In the last twenty years, technology has changed quite a bit. But what you've seen in the last twenty years will pale in comparison to the changes we'll face in the next twenty years.

THE MICROCHIP

Go ahead and take this short quiz. You'll find a microchip in:

a) your personal home computer
b) a nuclear warhead
c) your new, digital clock radio
d) your new car
e) a & b
f) all of the above

The best answer is "all of the above." The microchip is everywhere. In short order it might seem that the only place you won't find a microchip is your fish tank—and who knows? Bill Gates and Intel are probably working on that.

Since the invention of the microchip, manufacturers have found economical, valuable uses for them. They keep electronic devices running smoothly and make them run better. The microchip has also accelerated how fast technology is introduced. Computers work faster than ever. People become more productive. Information is shared faster. And the end result is tens of thousands of new products released to the public each year.

WHAT'S COMING?

There was a day when people had never heard of a microwave and they didn't know what the initials V-C-R stood for *(was it Video Cactus Recorder?)*. No one knows for sure what new technology the next hundred years will bring, but it's exciting to see the changes already taking place and to imagine even more.

FASTER COMPUTERS

Computers are doubling in speed every eighteen months while their prices continue to fall. The computer could become the central command area for your home—adjusting the temperature and turning on the lights when you come home. It will read the paper to you and understand your voice (who will need a primitive mouse?). It's possible that we're a

THE BOTTOM LINE

News Media

A growing number of people already get their news on the Internet. The day will come when you'll never wait up just to watch the 10:00 nightly news. You can already watch **CNN** on demand via the Internet. Soon you'll be able to listen to your customized newscast while driving in your car.

generation away from people who will hardly ever use pen and paper.

CATCH A CLUE

Watch Your Future

Have you been bitten by the futurist bug? You can read more on the future and enjoy some speculation at a number of websites. These websites aren't Christian, but they do hold lots of information.

Watch a sample video of a 1998 Keynote to a World Sales Conference of a Top 10 Software company, entitled "Beyond 2001: The Shape of Things to Come" by going to http://www.isbspeakers.com/WebVideo/Hiemstra.ram.

Listen to a 1998 speech on future implications for education by going to http://198.239.32.144/ramgen/199804/1998040010B.ra.

Listen to a 1997 speech on future implications for the environment by going to http://198.239.32.144/ramgen/199701/1997010004A.ra.

The World Future Society is a nonprofit educational and scientific organization for people interested in how social and technological developments are shaping the future. With 30,000 members, the Society serves as a nonpartisan clearinghouse for ideas about the future, including forecasts, recommendations, scenarios, alternatives, and more. http://www.wfs.org/

Here's a site that talks about doing business in the future. http://www.herman.net/archive.html

How about joining in on a discussion on cloning? http://www.globalchange.com/clone_index.htm

Interested in predictions of life in the next millennium? http://www.globalideasbank.org/ http://www.technotouch.com/mindshare.html

continued from previous page
Here are some other pages to check out:
http://21net.com/home/welcome.htm
http://www.futurist.com
http://www.globalchange.com/main.htm
http://www.planet-tech/community/scans_public.asp

TELECOMMUNICATIONS

Wireless phones are fast becoming commonplace. Videophones exist in crude form already and will undoubtedly become better, economical, and widespread. Of course, the downside of this is that telecommuters will be forced to shower and shave. Soon after that, hologram phones will force them to get *completely* dressed.

ONLINE COMMERCE

Parents of teenage girls: Beware! The mall is not your only danger spot anymore. Your kids can buy almost anything at 3 A.M.—in whatever color they like and have it shipped anywhere they like. In your lifetime, you're likely to buy almost everything—including your groceries—on-line.

MEDICAL WONDERS

Just a few years ago the life expectancy in the United States was about seventy-six years. The medical community is beginning to think that most of us could live much longer. With medical advances in genetic science and microbiology, we could all live longer. Children born today are likely to live beyond the twenty-first century. No one can really predict an accurate life expectancy for a child born today. (But don't expect another Methuselah—969 years old may be expecting a little too much.)

WOW!

They Said What?

"There is no reason anyone would want a computer in their home."—**Ken Olson, President & Founder, Digital Equipment, 1977;**

"Who would ever want to hear actors talk?"
—**H.M. Warner, Warner Bros., 1927;**

"Louis Pasteur's theory of germs is ridiculous fiction."
—**Pierre Pachet, Professor of Physiology, Toulouse, 1872;**

"I think there is a world market for maybe five computers."
—**Thomas Watson, Chairman of IBM, 1943;**

"Heavier than air flying machines are impossible."
—**Lord Calvin, Royal Society, 1895;**

"Stocks have reached what looks like a permanently high plateau."
—**Irving Fisher, Prof. Economics, Yale Univ., 1929;**

"640K ought to be enough for anybody."
—**Bill Gates, 1981.**

TRANSPORTATION

The electric car was introduced in the 1990s but it held little appeal because it had limited range and speed. Hybrid cars are being developed that will have both an improved internal combustion engine and electric engine, allowing for the best of both worlds. Even the internal combustion engines will improve so that combined with its electric counterpart, your miles per gallon will greatly improve. Add to the list of options a hydraulic-powered engine, and we might kick the gasoline habit completely.

Cars will be programmed to remember regularly traveled routes. They'll know when to turn on your blinker and be able to sense other cars on the road. Who knows, maybe "autopilot" will replace cruise control.

SOCIAL CHANGES

You've probably heard the words "modern" and "postmodern" being passed around. These are words used to describe some of the social changes that are happening today. In short it means this: We don't think, learn, or act like we used to. People living today think differently and make decisions differently than they did in 1975.

These changes lead to shifts in society's values and interests.

A Voice from the Grave

"Books on the twentieth or twenty-first century are getting to be so numerous that the whole subject will soon be a deadly bore."
—*The Literary World*, 1890

WOW!

In some ways, our society is still changing. In other ways, the shift has already occurred.

CHURCH

In the first half of the twentieth century, religion—namely the Christian church—was in vogue. It seems that almost everyone grew up knowing about God and knowing about the Bible. Most Christians read their Bible and knew classic Bible stories. Much of that has changed. The Barna research group says that now one out of three people is "unchurched" (not attended a church service in the last six months). The younger the people, the less likely they are to be in church. Forty percent of eighteen to twenty-nine-year-olds have not been to church in the last six months.

These people are not necessarily abandoning religion. Some still read their Bible regularly and listen to Christian radio, but they're dropping out of church because they don't see it as important or relevant. Barna comments, "The American public is sending a clear message to Christian leaders: Make Christianity accessible and practical or don't expect their participation."

Whether they know it or not, churches are dealing with this change right now. As the church enters the new millennium, it needs to decide how to deal with some major changes in perspective.

Defined and Defining Culture

The Internet is the perfect invention for the Age of Information—it also propagates it. With the Internet on hand, few pieces of information—good or bad—are outside of reach.

GOD AND THE INTERNET

Barna predicts that by the year 2010, 10 to 20 percent of U.S. citizens will be getting their entire religious experience through the Internet.

BRAND LOYALTY

For generations, denominations were a part of the family heritage. Many people were born, baptized, married, and buried in the same church. Their children usually followed suit. Born a Presbyterian, always a Presbyterian. Born a Methodist, always a Methodist.

Most pastors will tell you that this loyalty no longer exists. In a previous era, Christians were loyal to their church and loyal to their denomina-

---

Christianity Online?

THE BOTTOM LINE

What's Christian about the internet? Plenty. Here are a few interesting sites to explore.

Devotions on line:
http://www.devotionals.net/

http://searchopolis.com/rd/dia/devotions/http://www.provide.net/~dragl/devo.htm

http://searchopolis.com/rd/dia/devotions/http://www.raleighfirstag.org/rs-devotions.htm

http://searchopolis.com/rd/dia/devotions/http://almosthome.nu/hiddentreasure/devo/committment.html

Listen to Christian radio broadcasts:
http://www.icrn.com

Sample of a Church with a great web presence:
http://www.saddleback.org

An index of churches with web pages:
http://www.best.com/~nodakid/church.html

A Christian community and great resource:
http://www.christianity.net

tion. Now such loyalties rarely exist. Many people shop for a church based on beliefs, worship style, and fellowship.

WHAT'S A CHURCH TO DO?

There are many ways churches respond. See the section entitled "Advanced Lifesaving" for more on this subject.

Stay Sharp

While no one knows for sure, it's safe to guess that one third of the jobs that will appear in the classifieds in the year 2025 have not been invented yet.

WOW!

THE INTERNET

Before the 1990s, few people had heard of the Internet. And while some were still enjoying the revolution of the Commodore 64 and the floppy disk, the Internet suddenly emerged and left everything else choking in its dust.

Communities

Whether it's http://www.christianity.net or http://www.yahoo.com or http://www.msnbc.com, many on-line companies are working hard to build a community. They're recruiting people with similar interests who keep coming back to their site again and again. Maybe they come back to chat. Maybe for research. Maybe to surf. The point is, they come back—again and again. And when they do they feel like they're coming home and are among friends. Think of it as *Cheers* for the new millennium.

Starting Young
Internet users are starting young. Many young people growing up today will not know life before the Internet any more than you know life apart from the lightbulb. The Barna Research Group (http://www.barna.com) cites that one half of all teens use the Internet for casual relationships and interaction, through chat rooms. And one out of every three teenagers uses the Internet to make new friendships. And with the growing number of web sites just for kids, the Internet holds appeal for even the youngest users.

EXPERIENCE KNOCKSOUT LOGIC

Why does McDonald's outmarket Burger King? Most adults would agree that Burger King's food *tastes* better. McDonald's isn't necessarily healthier or cheaper. So why does McDonald's win? It wins because it is a better *experience*. For years, McDonald's has made itself the *fun* place to get fast food. Burger King, on the other hand, concentrated on taste. Burger King sells food, McDonald's sells an experience—and McDonald's wins.

McDonald's understands one of the major hallmarks in the shift from modern to postmodern thinking. One of the major differences is that people have moved from linear learning (A+B=C) to experiential learning *(If I can feel it, it's true).*

These changes impact more than fast-food choices. Moral choices, values, and religion are all determined first by experience, then by logic. If you still have a *modern* mind-set, the shift doesn't make sense to you. But that is your *logic* showing through. Whether you like the change or not, it's already taken place.

Church Music Example

One way to illustrate this shift is through the example of a church worship leader. A modern worship leader might want to use old hymns to pass them on to a new generation. But a postmodern worship leader says "It is not my job to teach people what is 'good church music.' It is my job to help people have an experience of God" (quote from Leonard Sweet's book *SoulTsunami*).

WOW!

Was He Right?

"If there is one point on which both secular forecasters and inspired mystics agree, it is that during the brief two and a half decades separating us from the year 2000, the present world order will undergo a total change."—*Omar V. Garrison*, **Encyclopedia of Prophecy (1978)**

INTERACTION RULES

Another major shift in our society involves a move from the passive to the interactive. Rather than sit and take in information, people today want to touch it and manipulate it. They want to *experience* it. That's one reason Internet use is climbing and television watching is declining.

Learning and School Affected

When you went to school you probably sat, absorbed facts, and recited them for a test. Today schools teach differently. They create "learning environments." Today's students sit in small, interactive groups, partici-pate in workshops, and participate in exercises where they discover the truth. The best teachers today don't *lecture*, they *facilitate*.

Put in a CD-ROM

When CD-ROMs first came installed in computers, software companies scrambled to throw whatever they could onto a CD-ROM. For the first generation of reference products, whatever company produced the most information on a CD was the winner. It didn't matter how the material was organized or how well you could search it. It was only important that it was on the CD.

Then came *Microsoft Encarta*.

Encarta wasn't just information; it was interactive information—and it was fun. You could watch video clips, see pictures, listen to sounds. It wasn't just a dump of information; it was both educational and entertain-ing. Just a few years after the first CD-ROM, an entire software category now exists called "Edu-Tainment."

MONEY, JOBS, AND THE ECONOMY

One thing that is not changing is that we're still a consumer-oriented society. But the way that people shop will be different. You used to shop between the hours of

WOW!

Job Security Is Gone

"Fifty percent of the jobs in the classified ads won't even be around ten years from now."
—Leonard Sweet

nine to five during the weekday or maybe a little longer on the weekend. The Internet is changing that, too. You can buy almost anything on the Internet twenty-four hours a day, seven days a week, any day of the year—including Thanksgiving and Christmas.

Customized Stores

Ever walk into a music store and try to decide between two CDs? You hold one in each hand and have trouble deciding which to buy. Or have you ever walked into a gift store and wanted to buy a teddy bear but didn't like any of the options they carried? You liked the fur on one but the clothes on the other, right?

WIDE ANGLE

A New Century

"A new century is to a nation very much what a new year is to a man."
—poet Paul Valery, December 1900

A new wave of interactive shopping has emerged. You can customize music CDs for about the same cost as buying one in a store. Do you want the best, recent releases from Garth, Shania, and Amy but don't want to buy all three albums? Shop at http://www.musicmaker.com and you can order your CD with the songs *you* want. They'll customize your own CD of various artists and mail it to you.

This kind of interaction is not just on the Internet. Some gift stores are selling "make your own" items like teddy bears. *You* pick the outfit. *You* pick the size. Make it *your* way.

MICROMARKETING

Back in the olden days of 1980, companies devoted their advertising dollars to the "mass market." They bought TV ads that reached everyone. They installed billboards that everyone could see. They invested in magazine advertising that reached millions.

Today, many are practicing "micromarketing." Big companies can reach a distinct market and unique niche through directed, Internet advertising. Do you have a product you'd like to market to left-handed men with beards? The Internet has the community you need.

A DIFFERENT WORLD

The United States used to be isolationist. It never can be again. Future leaders might want it to be and future presidents might try to be, but we can never go back. Businesses are global. Corporations manufacture and sell all over the world. Every nation's economy is impacted by other nations. If the Asian stock market takes a plunge, Europe follows. If Europe does well, the U.S. market will respond.

THE INTERNET STRIKES AGAIN

Visit a chat room. Play an on-line game. Go to a message board. Most likely you'll find people interacting from all over the world. The Internet makes everyone a neighbor. It doesn't matter where two people live—the Internet brings them together.

THE DEMOGRAPHICS OF THE NEW WORLD

Remember Disney's "It's a small world, after all?" If you went on that ride, you sat in a boat and rode through unique, odd cultures. Each probably seemed fairly foreign to you. Most likely, if you're not a minority now, you will be.

Again, futurist Leonard Sweet illustrates this change very well when he says: "If we could shrink the earth's population to a village of 100 people, it would look like this:

- 57 Asians, 21 Europeans, 14 North and South Americans, and 8 Africans;
- 70 would be non-white;
- 70 would be non-Christian;
- 70 would be unable to read;
- 50 would suffer from malnutrition;
- 80 would live in substandard housing;
- 1 would have a college education;
- 50 percent of the entire world wealth would be in the hands of 6 people;
- All 6 people would be citizens of the U.S."

SECTION 5
NEW CLOTHES FOR AN OLD BODY

HOW TO PREPARE YOUR CHURCH FOR THE NEW MILLENNIUM

IT'S LIKE STARTING A DIET

Beginnings are always difficult. Beginning a diet. That's a tough one. Beginning a savings account. Another toughie. What about beginning the church? Easy, right? All you've got to do is get people together, grab a guitar player, find someone to preach, and have at it. Right?

The new millennium comes with a new smell. It's an opportunity to relight a fire for reaching people. It's the perfect opportunity for a new beginning for your church.

Why Change?

Giving was higher last year. The ladies' Bible study even increased in attendance. If you're thinking that the new millennium *doesn't* offer you a chance to catch your breath and change the way church is done, answer the following questions:

• How many people committed their lives to Christ last year?

_____

_____

_____

_____

_____

_____

• How many *new* people committed to be regular volunteers?

_____

_____

_____

_____

_____

• Did giving increase? How much? How did giving to missions do?

_____

_____

_____

_____

_____

_____

• Did attendance increase or decrease last year? By how much?

_____

_____

_____

_____

_____

_____

• Do the people in your church get together regularly because they *want* to get together?

_____

_____

_____

_____

_____

_____

• What's the average age of your congregation? Younger than forty? Younger than thirty?

_____

_____

_____

_____

_____

_____

If after you've taken that little test you feel encouraged about your church—wonderful! Be encouraged. Take a vacation!

But if, after answering those questions, you have one of those sinking feelings, it's time for a change.

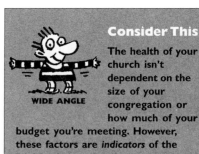

WIDE ANGLE

Consider This

The health of your church isn't dependent on the size of your congregation or how much of your budget you're meeting. However, these factors are *indicators* of the health of your church.

GOING SHOPPING FOR A LEMON

No one wants to go out shopping for something that *doesn't* work. Imagine walking into a car dealership and asking for a car that's guaranteed to break down in three years, leak oil, and need new tires every five thousand miles.

There's a lot to consider when you step out and attempt to change a church. And it's easy to end up with ideas that just don't work. Before we mention all of the right things you should do, here are a few things you should avoid.

- AVOID the temptation to consider what other churches are doing and adopt their programming. Success in the new millennium will be marked by those churches who know their target audience. The church up the street from you that is growing so fast that the building is busting at the seams is doing things that you might not be able to.

- AVOID dropping a new idea or program in the lap of your church and expect them to grab at it with enthusiasm that rivals yours. It's easier to sway one person at a time than it is to persuade groups of people.

- AVOID doing *anything* until you've committed your ideas to serious prayer. The often-used phrase "Have you prayed about it?" has caused many of us to consider prayer something to fit in after we've made our decision. We're eager to pray and ask God to bless our decision, but oftentimes slow to ask God to shape the decision He's calling us to make.

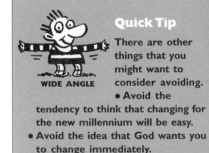

Quick Tip

WIDE ANGLE

There are other things that you might want to consider avoiding.

- Avoid the tendency to think that changing for the new millennium will be easy.
- Avoid the idea that God wants you to change immediately.
- Avoid the temptation to change quickly. Sometimes going slowly is a good idea.

DON'T MESS WITH THE STUFF, MAN!

Sure, changing is neat. But, remember that some things ought not to be touched. When you set out to make some big changes in your church, you have to approach the task with the same fear that you did when you entered the room your parents kept only for company. (You remember that room, don't you? It's the one your mom got upset with you about if you even thought about taking your Legos into.)

So, there are two things that you shouldn't mess with when you change.

Theology

Whether you're Baptist, Methodist, Episcopalian, or Independent, your theology makes you distinct. It gives your church its personality. But it's so much more.

Your theology defines how you think about Christ. It demonstrates

WIDE ANGLE

Tell Me More . . .

Want a border guideline on what's essential for your church? Consider the Apostles' Creed. It's not "Scripture", but it does give you a guideline for what's important.

I believe in God
the Father Almighty
Maker of heaven and earth.
And in Jesus Christ
His only Son our Lord,
Who was conceived by the Holy Spirit,
Born of the Virgin Mary,
Suffered under Pontius Pilate,
Was crucified, dead and buried;
He descended into hell;
The third day He rose again from the dead;
He ascended into heaven,
And sits on the right hand of God the Father Almighty;
From thence he shall come to judge the living and the dead.
I believe in
The Holy Spirit;
The Holy Catholic Church;
The Communion of Saints;
The forgiveness of sins;
The resurrection of the body;
And the life everlasting.

the edges of your belief as well as the core. We don't have to tell you how important it is. But it's easy to slip up and mess with the basis of who you are as you set out to change what you do.

Remember: What you believe makes you who you are—not necessarily what you do.

The Truth of the Gospel

God has called everyone who believes in Him to go out and reach unbelievers. We have Good News to share. But God hasn't given us a blueprint on how we are supposed to go about it. Keep the truth about spreading the gospel but feel comfortable changing the format.

Okay, so we've warned you of what not to do when you approach the idea of a change. But, what should you do? Where do you start? What do you do to prepare for the future? It begins with a micro/macro look at the way you're already heading.

MACRO CHURCH-O-NOMICS

Microscopes are great for looking at the detail in a blood cell. But you can't put a microscope on the bow of a ship and navigate your way to land. Likewise, trying to count the number of white blood cells with a periscope will make you crazy. In other words, both are essential for discovering things. In the same way, in preparing your church for the new millennium you'll need both macro and micro tools.

Let's get macroscopic for a few minutes. Take a step back with us and let's look at the church. What is it's purpose? Why does it exist?

The Bible gives a good description of the church. Well, actually it gives a good description of what the early church was, what it did, and how it operated. The simplest description is found in Acts 2:42-47.

They devoted themselves to the apostles' teaching, and to the fellowship, to the breaking of bread and to prayer. Everyone was filled with awe, and many wonders and miraculous signs were done by the apostles. All the believers were together and had everything in common. Selling their possessions and goods, they gave to anyone as he had need. Every day they continued to meet together in the temple courts. They broke bread in their homes and ate together with glad and sincere hearts, praising God and enjoying the favor of all the people. And the Lord added to their number daily those who were being saved.

So, what do you get from this passage? Here's what we got: There's some stuff that the church did, does, and should always do. What can we learn from Acts?

1. They devoted themselves to the apostles' teaching.
2. They devoted themselves to fellowship.
3. They devoted themselves to eating together.
4. They devoted themselves to prayer.
5. They were used for miraculous signs and wonders.
6. They sold their stuff and gave away the money.

So, what you just read was the rule of order for the early church. Now, speaking "macroly" for a moment, did you notice any of the following?

1.They used a high-tech computer-driven setup to draw people or communicate their message.
2.They formed committees to decide the color of the carpeting in the new Family Life Center.
3.They built a coffeehouse and hired hot Christian bands to use as a draw for evangelism.
4.They strategized and built a global television network in hopes of reaching the entire world before the year 400 A.D.

Nope. You didn't read any of that. Acts describes the central core of the church—but it doesn't prescribe how that core set of values was to be accomplished. It lays out the goal without laying out the steps to reaching it. It was part of God's awesome plan to give us the essentials and then leave the rest to us. He decides the message; we tweak the medium.

Micro-organizing

What you're going to have to do for the next few pages is unusual. We'd like you to read and write a bit, then we're going to ask you to do some page flipping to check some essential ministry spots. Just sit back, follow the directions, and we'll do the rest.

First, let's look at what you're already doing.

Question #1: You probably live within a congregation of—people, right? Those people have needs. How do you know their needs? How do those needs get met? (Do you meet their needs; Do you have a team of people? Do you ignore their needs?)

_____

_____

_____

_____

_____

_____

Question #2: What is your worship like? Do you use an organ? Does the speaker wear a suit? Is there a sermon? Do you provide pillows for people who tithe more than 10 percent?

_____

_____

_____

_____

_____

_____

Question #3: This one might take some research. How do people describe your worship services? Slow, exciting, worshipful, unorganized, powerful, disturbing?

_____

_____

_____

_____

_____

_____

Question #4: What are the relationships in your church like? Are there small groups? Do people get together outside of the church to enjoy being together?

_____

_____

_____

_____

_____

_____

_____

You've done marvelous! Give yourself a hand. Now, we'd like you to read on. As you read, remember the answers you gave to these questions. We'll stop you from time to time and encourage you to look at what you wrote, then evaluate it based on some trends for the new millennium.

The Shape of Things That Are
One of the most startling facts about the church is that what we're doing now isn't because our church boards have decided to follow some set of holy regulations cemented by a governing body. In fact, most of the rules that we have for what we do in the church are the result of several people reading the Bible and saying, "Hey, this is what I get out of this, what do you think?" And then it goes from there. Here are a few things to remember.

1. **The style of worship isn't dictated by the Bible.** God never tells us what instruments to use, when to celebrate Communion, what the speaker should wear, and on and on.
2. **The day that we worship isn't pronounced in the Bible.** Sure, it's absolutely essential that believers gather for worship, but the Bible doesn't say that it has to be Sunday.
3. **Rules for membership aren't outlined by God.** In fact, it's rather difficult to find requirements for membership to a church in the Bible.

Stepping Outside the Box

The history of the church has led us to one of the most spectacular, lavishly decorated boxes in history. Within that box we've decided that everything that we've lived with throughout the history (or as long as we remember it) of the church is the way it's supposed to be. But history has led us to a dead end. Those who study history will tell you that the way the church is now is not the way it's always been. In the not too distant past, women weren't allowed to sit on the same side of the church as the men. People weren't allowed to smile because they were supposed to be somberly contemplating the Scriptures.

The process that all churches must undergo in the new millennium will be one of doing something with the box that tradition has left us with. How well will you do at this? Let's try something. We're going to give you a series of dots below. Your task is to connect all of the dots with four straight lines and without lifting your pencil! (The following exercise is taken from John Maxwell's book *Developing the Leader within You.)*

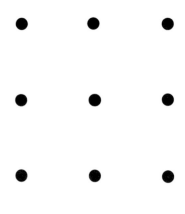

The answer may have stymied you. Maxwell writes, "You made certain assumptions about the problem that limited your range of answers. Did you assume the lines could not extend beyond the imaginary square formed by the dots? Break that assumption and you can solve the puzzle more easily.

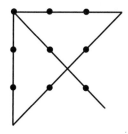

"This creative solution is fairly commonplace. Less well-known are alternate solutions that stem from breaking other assumptions, such as these suggested by astronomer Tom Wujec: Assumption: The lines must pass through the center of the dots. If you draw lines that just touch the dots, you can solve the puzzle in just three strokes:

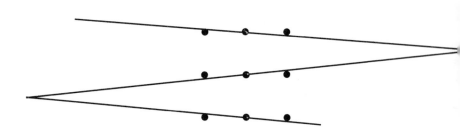

"Assumption: the Lines Must be thin. Connect the lines with one fat line to solve the problem"

"Assumption: You may not crease the paper. Fold the Paper twice so the dots all are together on the surface, and you need only one wide line.

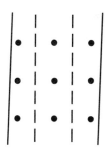

"Or how about these other ideas: 'Assumption: The paper must be flat. Roll the paper into a tube. It's possible to connect the dots with a spiral.

Or

"Assumption: You cannot rip the paper. Tear the paper into nine pieces with one dot on each, and connect all the dots by poking a hole through all the dots with your pencil."

So, what did you learn? Thinking outside the box is tough. Thinking outside the box takes time, resources, willingness, and an ability to even rearrange the parameters a bit. In the new millennium, three types of churches will emerge that will be known as people who deal with "the box" of tradition.

REDECORATORS

Churches that don't effectively know how to deal with the new millennium will take a look at the box that they're in with vigor. They'll decide that what they've been doing isn't working. But they'll fail to effectively strategize new ways to reach out, redesign, and rebuild their walls. In effect, these churches will simply redecorate their surroundings. They'll follow what other churches are doing. Buy media equipment. Build something new on their vacant land. They'll have everything in place to make it look like they're in step with the new millennium.

DECONSTRUCTORS

Churches who see the change coming, but don't know how to handle it will fall into this category. Just what is a deconstructing church? It's one that takes an alternate stand against the trends of the new millennium and make it their enemy.

Interestingly enough, deconstructing churches can do very well. They serve as havens for people who aren't comfortable with messing with tradition. They draw people back to an earlier time in church when they were growing up. And while every church that seeks to draw believers together for celebration and instruction are indispensable, deconstructing churches aren't on the cusp of the new millennium. And we can tell that you want to be on the cusp ('cause you're still reading!).

REBUILDERS

The rebuilding church for the new millennium will be one that embraces the current trend and does whatever it can to develop programming around it. These churches won't necessarily be the megachurches that you're hearing about. They'll be bent on reaching people in ways that are in step with the people they're trying to reach. They aren't interested in redecorating their boxes. Rather, they'll feel comfortable tossing out the old for the sake of the effective.

Rebuilding the church for the new millennium takes a knowledge of what's happening. It requires you to step out and learn as much about the new era as you can. It begins with a study of what tons of trend watchers call postmodernism.

POST-WHO?

When the clock hits midnight striking a new year, the law of gravity won't change. The speed limit will be the same. But, already, people who look into the future of the church and prognosticate the things to come are telling us that the future of the church is found in targeting people called "postmoderns." Some give specific dates, saying that postmoderns are people born after 1980. Others portray a postmodern mind-set that must be understood and targeted. What is postmodernity? Who are postmoderns? What do they believe? Try this simple quiz to get your learning jump-started.

A POST-POP TRUE OR FALSE QUIZ

• *Postmoderns are people who are comfortable with regular change.*

True. In fact, postmoderns love change. They welcome it. But, they welcome a change for a purpose rather than a change just for the sake of changing.

• *Postmoderns enjoy being in their homes. They enjoy solitude. They have few relationships with their neighbors.*

True and false. While postmoderns love being in their homes, they thrive on outdoor sports and even extreme sports.

• *Because of their love of individuality and solitude, postmoderns don't enjoy being around people.*

False. Postmoderns THRIVE on things like relationships and community. They long to be a part of a group while still maintaining their individuality within that group.

• *Postmoderns don't care about spirituality. They're suspicious about Christianity. They care little about Jesus.*

True and False. Postmoderns are deeply spiritual and are on a search for truth. They love the concept of Jesus, but they're suspicious of Christians.

• *Postmodernity is a reaction to modernity. A time when people felt that science and reason held the keys to knowledge.*

True. Postmodernity is a striving towards finding truth through emotion and discussion.

Now, take just a few minutes and read back over the four questions in the "Micro-Organizing" section a few page back. How does the information you just gleaned shape your understanding of how the church body ought to relate to each other? How does it help you understand how worship might be made more effective? Spend a few minutes reading back through the quiz and the questions to shape your thinking.

POSTMODERNITY IS COMING ALIVE

Leonard Sweet is a Dean at Drew University. He's an author, historian, and futurist. He outlines the hallmark of the burgeoning generation that has already made its appearance. Through his analysis, he outlines the following hallmarks of the postmodern mentality.

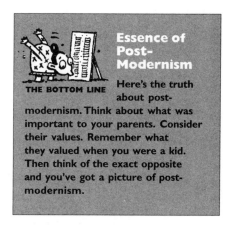

Essence of Post-Modernism

THE BOTTOM LINE Here's the truth about postmodernism. Think about what was important to your parents. Consider their values. Remember what they valued when you were a kid. Then think of the exact opposite and you've got a picture of postmodernism.

1. Authority is a thing of the past.

Postmoderns don't look to authority as someone to be listened to. The authority in their lives is the relationship. Gone are the days when authority figures dispense information. Rather, those who are seen as the authority are to be studied so they can shape the way we use information.

2. The Borg.

The postmodern mind-set thinks connectedness. It desires to be a part of a group without losing individuality. This is a contrast from recent history. In the distant past conformity was the norm. Then, individuality was necessary. In the new era, people will desire individuality so long as they can be part of a group of *individuals.*

3. The almighty experience.

It isn't enough to tell someone that the truth is the truth. They must feel that it is the truth. The mantra of the postmodern person is "If I feel it, it's true." Nuff said.

4. The person is the brand.

In the past, people attached themselves to "brands" such as Hoover (for vacuum cleaners). They looked for brands to give their approval to and considered the brand names sufficient enough backing to drop their hard-earned cash. These days, things sell on the basis of who's associated with it. Consider Air Jordans and Martha Stewart.

5. Extremism.

Doing things dangerously is the new theme. It's not enough that we're going mountain biking. Let's add a twist. Let's go mountain biking off a cliff. We'll pull out parachute cords, drift in our canoes, drop our packs and whitewater down the rapids and over the falls.

Hit the brakes again for a moment. How does this info help you see your church? What information can you take from this section that will shape some of the changes you'll be making in your church in the new millennium?

Okay. So you're fed up with the history lesson and the quizzes. What can you do to face the new millennium head-on?

TELL STORIES

Here's a contrast for ya. A sermon is a linear thing. It has a beginning, some points, and a conclusion. It might include an illustration or two. It might tap into your emotions. It might even move you to a decision. Now for the contrast.

When was the last time you heard a good story? Maybe it was a long joke. Possibly something you heard on the elevator on your way to your cubicle. Chances are that you remember the most recent story you heard before you remember the sermon. Why?

Stories engage us. They move us. They aren't linear. And a good story told well evokes emotion, senses, and causes us to get involved in what's going on.

WIDE ANGLE

What's The Essence of a Good Story? Every Story Has:

● **A way to draw people into the story.** This is usually done at the beginning of the story with an element of the fantastic, humorous, or unusual.

● **A powerful plot.** When you tell a story, remember that you need to weave it like a strong basket. It needs to connect together.

● **A strong point.** Stories told without a point make the listeners feel like they've wasted their time. Stories with a meaningful point cause the listeners to possibly make a decision or change their minds on a subject.

● **Stories told well usually connect with real-life experiences.** They use real places, real people, or real situations.

The story café

Consider organizing times when your church can get together, drink coffee, and tell stories. Have volunteers come prepared to share their stories, and then have a scheduled speaker who has prepared something really unique and well thought out.

Story sermons
If you have an ability telling stories, consider not preaching for a service. Tell a good story from the Bible. Use color by describing who different characters might have been and what they might have been like. Include pictures projected on overhead or even copied and passed around (If you pass pictures make sure you have enough for everyone).

Storytime at worship
There are several Christian professional storytellers making the circuit. Hire one for a Sunday service.

Use the best story of all—your life
With the unconnectedness that's rampant today, tell people who you are. When you've told them, stop talking. In other words, don't say "That's my story, now what you need to decide. . .do. . .choose. . .change. . . " Instead, just tell them what you've experienced and let the story go.

BUILD COMMUNITY

Building community is something the church has been doing for a while now. And, we've been doing it mostly out of a reaction to the lack of community many are experiencing. But adding a sense of community in the new millennium has a different twist. Instead of providing community because it's lacking, consider adding it because it's something that we're beginning to value as an essential element.

Think about the society that we live in. Houses are getting bigger. In subdivisions, on any given day, people are leaving early in the morning and not returning until late at night. More day care has kept children from developing neighborhood friendships.

And then there's cyberspace. With the onset of the Internet, community as we know it has become a thing of the past. Community is now defined in a different way—by how many people are on your buddy list and how many people fill your E-mail address book.

But with these realities, the church stands in a strategic position to develop a new sense of community. By the time you're finished reading this book, the number of Internet connections and personal computers in homes has doubled and possibly tripled. How can the church look into the future and develop a millennial community?

Church chat
Develop your own church web site and host monthly chats for church attenders only. Better yet, if you have a larger church, consider hosting age-level chats on different nights throughout the month.

Newsletters
Print media isn't a dinosaur. It isn't going to be obsolete anytime soon. However, technology has conditioned some of us on how we read and process information. Consider E-mailing your church newsletter or even posting it on your church's website.

Church-wide events
Because we're building larger homes and are barricading ourselves from others using technology, there's a new drive to get out and get connected. It might sound like an ironic twist, but the more people are isolating

themselves by choice, the more they're driven to get connected with other humans. Host church campouts. Have holiday cook-outs. Do whatever you can to get people connected with each other.

Small Groups

These are more essential now than ever before. They've existed for a while, but for the new millennium they need to be redefined. In short, use small groups to provide community. However, consider the various types when you organize yours.

New believers groups

Established for the care and feeding of baby Christians.

Local groups

Established for people who want to know people who live close to them.

Study groups

Designed for in-depth study of a book or topic.

Age groups

For people who want to hang out with others who are having the same experiences in life.

Support groups

For people who need advice from others who have similar experiences.

The list of groups is endless. Remember the purpose—community.

THE EXPERIENCE

In modern times, science and reason hold the keys to knowledge and understanding. The future of the church rests in understanding that postmodern keys to knowledge are in the experience. But planning and pulling off an experience isn't about having a large screen filled with projected images that move the audience. It's about creating meaningful experiences that move people to a decision and action.

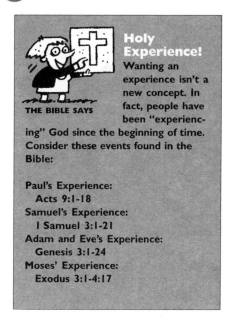

THE BIBLE SAYS

Holy Experience! Wanting an experience isn't a new concept. In fact, people have been "experiencing" God since the beginning of time. Consider these events found in the Bible:

Paul's Experience:
  Acts 9:1-18
Samuel's Experience:
  I Samuel 3:1-21
Adam and Eve's Experience:
  Genesis 3:1-24
Moses' Experience:
  Exodus 3:1-4:17

- **The worship experience.**
  Worship is and should always be a planned time when we gather together to celebrate God and our relationship with Him. However, the entire experience of worship can be formulated to impact the audience in an entirely sensory way. Consider having video clips, pictures, graphs, and announcements all coordinated to match parts of the service. Also consider having one person who crafts your worship *instead* of several people who plan different elements. It might be as simple as asking someone gifted in planning worship to oversee the people who plan the separate elements. Having one person looking out for the experience ensures that everything fits tightly together.
- **The pastoral experience.** Since society is quickly becoming more unconnected with a stronger desire to get more connected, what do you

do? Make pastoring an experience. How do you do that?

Visitation. Visitation is quickly becoming a lost art. While people feel invaded by the pastor who stops in for a cup of tea and a chat, they welcome a pastor who comes bearing gifts. Consider making an excuse to visit people. Buy them gifts and take them to every person in your church.

PARTICIPATORY

Call it a new activism. Label it a desire to be involved in change. People in the new millennium will want to be involved. Through their desire for belonging and their eagerness to be a part of a community, they'll do anything to participate in making things better and more productive.

- **Make meaningful meetings productive.** Meetings get a bad rap— and rightly so. But consider giving people an active part in meetings. Assign people to research the community or to develop a new strategy for reaching people. Give people the option to help develop a ministry area.

INTERACTIVE

The change in teaching style happened a long time ago. New curriculums have led us to explore new ideas, like hands-on learning where students get involved with the topic through tactile or kinesthetic learning. And then there's interactive learning where students get involved in a Bible story, then teach each other what it means through a process of debriefing.

But in the new millennium, interaction will take on a whole new meaning. Beyond the classroom, there are the following concepts.

CATCH A CLUE

Making Things Interactive

So, you've got a home-run sermon, study, or small group lesson planned, but you want to make it interactive. How do you do that? Here are some ideas for making anything interactive:

Preaching: *Pass the microphone.* Give people a chance to respond to what you're saying. *Get in small groups.* It's okay to have people spend the last five minutes talking about what you just preached on. *Act on it.* After you preach, give people a piece of paper and have them write down one commitment they're willing to make as a result of your sermon. Then have them share that commitment with someone as they're leaving. *Let them learn from each other.* Spend the first part of your message speaking, then have people get in small groups. Ask a series of questions and allow groups to answer them.

Teaching: *Play a game.* Use a game to effectively drive your point home. Instead of teaching them on the barrier that sin creates, have them construct a wall out of bed pillows and try and communicate with each other. They won't be able to do it, and they'll learn how our communication with God is hindered when we sin. *Use small groups.* Just as in interactive preaching, it's okay to let students discuss and learn from each other. Give groups a task to do and then let them share their results with another group, then with the entire class. *Debrief.* The heart of effective interactive teaching uses solid debriefing questions. Create an experience, then ask them how that experience relates to the Bible passage.

- **Interactive preaching.** Ever listened to a group of teenagers talk about themselves? If you do you'll notice one thing very fast—they listen intently to whoever has the mike, or whoever is talking. People learn best from each other. Consider passing the mike during a sermon. Try using more powerpoints to drive the message of your sermon home. Turn the sermon into a Bible study time where EVERYONE gets in on the talking and you become the facilitator.

- **Interactive curriculum.** Use church curriculum that promotes active and interactive learning. Get your hands on books that cause children, youth, and even adults to step inside the Bible stories and search through them.

Be Intellectual

In the society that is quickly approaching, a sense of being and intellectualism will be highly valued. But consider another interesting twist. Intellectualism must be meshed with reality. Being an intellectual means that you've got the information, but you've also got the ability to apply it and describe it. How do you use this in your church?

- **Intellectual clubs.** Form groups of people who prepare discussions on different Bible truths and compare them with other belief systems. Then, host an evening at your church when these are presented.
- **Study.** Ask people in your congregation to join you in studying another religion. Be prepared to discuss why Christianity is better than another religion.

SECTION 6
ADVANCED LIFESAVING

HOW TO PRESENT THE GOSPEL TO A NEW WORLD

IMAGINE THIS...

You're standing at the water cooler catching a quick break before going back to make a few calls. You strike up a conversation with Ned who, based on your assessment of his lifestyle, hasn't a clue about who God is. You think to yourself that this guy could really use a dose of good, old-fashioned religion. You begin with a short description of sin, follow with several paragraphs about living forever with God, and conclude with one of those decision-making type of comments.

When you finish, Ned walks away. He never speaks to you again.

OR THIS...

You love mowing your lawn. In fact, you spent well over a thousand dollars to add extra bells and whistles to your riding lawn mower. You mow every week. Your neighbor's lawn is in need of serious care. In fact, his is the only lawn on the block that is unkempt. One beautiful Saturday morning you're out for a mow when your neighbor flags you down and asks if he can borrow your mower. "Mine has been on the fritz for weeks now, and I really need to mow today." he says. "In fact, the only time I've got is right now. What do you say?" You refuse, stating that it might be time for him to go buy a new mower and yours is way too nice to loan out. After sharing a few choice words, you drive off and he slams his door.

The two of you never speak again.

OR THIS...

You get to talking with a new attender at your church. After a few minutes of conversation, you discover that he isn't a believer yet, and that he's a computer whiz. You've been having some unusual problems with your computer that you can't fix. He offers to come over and take a look. Deep in the recesses of your mind you think that you might be able to evangelize this guy.

After a brief meal together, the two of you head off to the study. He immediately turns on your computer screen and asks if he can show you his web site. Once he fires up your web browser, a screen pops up—it's the last place you surfed. Let's just say that it's not the most wholesome place you've surfed. A few minutes of awkwardness pass as he fumbles through a quick tour of his site. Then, he unexpectedly hurries out the door.

You haven't seen him at church since.

THE BOTTOM LINE

Don't Feel Bad

You might have read the stories above and felt like those described your attempts at evangelism. Don't feel bad! Chances are, almost everyone who has tried to tell someone about Christ has met with peculiar, discouraging, and even disappointing results. Keep trying! Don't give up!

Evangelism. Never has anything been so important. And it so absolutely essential that we do it right. But, what's the right way to evangelize someone? And how will that change as we plant our feet firmly into the new millennium?

HAVE IT YOUR WAY

Before we go on, let's just take some time and discuss the way that you share Christ with others. How do you do it? Here's a situation.

You've known Ken for a couple of years now. He's been the best next-door neighbor you've ever had. You and Ken spend a lot of time together talking about your favorite hobby—investing. In fact, you've begun buying stock together in technology companies. The only drawback is that Ken is not a Christian. And, until tonight, Ken has stayed clear of that subject with you.

Tonight you and Ken get together briefly to discuss another stock you're planning on buying. After deciding to buy, Ken asks you why you attend church. It seems he's interested in going with you this Sunday.

You've got an open door to share your faith with Ken. What do you say? Write your response below.

_____

_____

_____

_____

_____

_____

So, what did you say? Did you wow him with your knowledge of the
Bible? Now consider this: How might people you know deal with the

CATCH A CLUE

Web Evangelism, Part I

Wonder how evangelism is being done on the web? Check
out these sites to find out.

http://www.brigada.org/today/articles/web-
evangelism.html

http://net.simplenet.com/
http://www.michelleakers.com/
http://homepages.enterprise.net/bcfgoodnews/
http://www.powertochange.com/
http://www.thegoal.com/
http://debate.org.uk/
http://www.daystarcom.org/
http://www.focus.org.uk/
http://sydney-christian.net/

situation? What about your pastor? How about your spouse? Does your answer compare with the way these people might answer?

We'd like you to gain some essential information on how evangelism might change in the new millennium. While a lot of the basics about evangelism won't change, the underpinnings of how evangelism gets accomplished in the new millennium will change drastically. Sit back and relax for the next few minutes. We're going to give you a quick tour of what's coming up in the new millennium. As you read, consider the response you wrote above. And consider how your response might change based on the information we've provided.

NOT CUT, NOT DRY

Evangelism in the new millennium will change. And like the centuries before the one we're approaching, effective evangelism will take time. Time to learn the new culture. Time to understand what strategies work best. And time to practice. Basically, it's not a cut-and-dried process. What worked before won't work in the future.

Bracing for the twenty-first century means throwing away all the methods that we feel might work in telling people about Jesus. Here's a quick overview of what doesn't work anymore.

THE ALMIGHTY LAWS

These laws aren't in the Bible, but for the longest time they proved to be the most effective method for persuading people to give their lives to Christ. The Four Spiritual Laws were a powerful idea—in fact, they still are. But more and more, people are confronted with the reality that few laws are unbreakable. A "law" for becoming a Christian? It just doesn't fit with the blurred boundaries that shape the new millennium.

Let's stop here. Was your answer for Ken similar to the way the Four Spiritual Laws are presented? Did you attempt to convince Ken by a series of statements aimed at convincing his intellect about his spiritual state?

KNOCK, KNOCK

Do you remember when wandering the neighborhoods and telling strangers about Jesus worked? It did, eons ago. These days, if you're lucky enough to find someone at home, you'll be even luckier if you can get them to open their door.

Eeek! Hit the brakes for a moment. Was your attempt to persuade Ken based on the friendship you'd gained with him over the years? Or, when you saw the open door, did you attempt to approach him like he has a disease that he needed cured? Were you a friend or a doctor?

CRUSADES

This one is *very* tricky. Christian crusades and revivals still mark the landscape of evangelism. And, many still work well. But consider that 80 percent of people who meet Jesus do so through a relationship with a friend. In the new millennium, crusades might possibly give way to big events that enable relationships rather than call for a decision immediately.

Was your discussion with Ken one that included an invitation to a revival, crusade,

WIDE ANGLE

Who Do You Know?

Do you know an unsaved person? Or are all of your friends saved, sanctified, spirit-filled soldiers for God? The best way to evangelize people who don't know Jesus is to get to know one person at a time. Begin forming relationships now. Then live like Christ among them and they just might begin to notice.

meeting with the pastor or another believer about his spiritual condition?

HI, I'M BOB, AND YOU'RE GOING TO HELL

Fire insurance is essential if you own a home. There was a time when people needed to know what hell was, and they needed to be informed about how to stay away from it. These days, most people have heard about hell. But because there are no absolutes, they write hell off as a myth or a place for the really evil people like Hitler. Ironically, there has been a resurgence of the belief in heaven. Unfortunately, it is accompanied with the false view that everyone goes to heaven, or at least the people who try to do good. Therefore, the logic goes that if they are basically good people, they don't have to worry about hell.

Did Ken get the feeling from you that he needed to decide right now—in spite of how much he really understood? Read back over the explanation that you gave him. Were you convinced or offended by what you might have told him? Was there love in your explanation, or did you approach him with cold hard facts about his eternity without Christ?

AH ONE, AND AH TWO, AND AH...

The church waded through a long time when saving the world was its one desire (and rightly so!). The result of that pursuit was keeping track of who decided what and when. Did they get the new Believers' Bible? Check. Did they sign up to join the church? Check. Cold number counting doesn't work anymore. While it's absolutely essential that we keep good track of where people are spiritually, it's also essential that the process doesn't become the only important thing.

How about your explanation to Ken? Read back through what you might have said. Was it motivated by a desire to see him rescued or by a desire to get a bragging point with other Christians? Or possibly by the desire to put another "notch" in your Bible?

CATCH A CLUE

Web Evangelism, Part II

Here are some more sites that are dedicated to evangelism on the web.

http://wri.leaderu.com/
http://www.womentodaymagazine.com/
http://www.whychrist.com/Admin/
http://www.actsweb.org/
http://www.geocities.com/Heartland/Flats/9740
http://www.geocities.com/~true_alien/
http://www.holyscriptures.com/jesusbanner.html
http://www.worldvillage.com/wv/square/chapel/safehaven/
http://www.completelyfreesoftware.com/
http://www.icnc.org/
http://www.grieving.org/
http://www.stonewallrevisited.com/
http://www.discovering-wisdom.com/
http://users2.ipa.net/~lturley/
http://website.lineone.net/~treasureseekers/
http://home.att.net/~charleswells/logismos/
http://www.christcom.net/iec/links.htm
http://www.newchristian.org/
http://www.missionaries.org/lifegate/gsps.html
http://www.jesusfilm.org/realvideo/
http://www.crusade.org/wto/ministry/

SLOGANS, JARGON, BRANDS

It used to be enough to say that you belonged to the First Church on the corner of Main and Chestnut. You used to be able to ask someone if they'd been saved by Jesus. But now, people are skeptical of slogans as a point of sale. They're equally unsure of shirts, cups, bracelets, shoelaces, hats, or bumper stickers that attempt to identify people groups. In short, don't rely on whatever you, your car, your kids, or even your dog is wearing to spread the gospel or open a door for evangelism.

Okay. Without slamming your description of what Christ did in your life, did you use "Christianese" as you spoke with Ken? Were you able to tell him the essentials of believing in Jesus without using words that he didn't understand?

WHAT CAN'T CHANGE

What cannot change as we enter a
new century? Okay, so you're ready
for a change. You're prepared for
the new millennium. Your bags are
packed. You're headed out the door.

Before you get too far down
the road, we'd like to caution you
about something. The face of
evangelism needs to change—but
the meat of it shouldn't be
touched. What shouldn't change?

WHO IS JESUS?

Millenialists have a plethora of
gods to choose from. Each one of
those false deities has a host of
people politicking for it. And, it's
easy, out of a desire to rescue
them, to give in and water down

WIDE ANGLE

Here's Something to Consider

If it's difficult for
you to remember
everything you'd
like to say to
someone about your relationship
with Christ, consider writing down
key ideas and putting them in your
wallet or purse. Better yet, arrange
your key ideas in an easily mem-
orizable format. Something like
"W.A.L.K." When I met Jesus I was
lost in sin. I Accepted him and my life
immediately changed. My Life since
then has been full of ups and downs.
my goal for the rest of my life is to
Keep walking with Jesus and consider
how I can live for Him every day.

the idea of who Jesus is and what He came to do. Jesus is God.

THE FALLEN NATURE OF HUMANITY

For some, being rescued is a foreign concept. These days, the lostness of humanity isn't something that's a real popular notion. But, a nonnegotiable in evangelism is that without the sacrifice of Jesus on the cross, we face an eternity in hell.

WE NEED JESUS

Once you've got a clear picture of who Jesus is and you've got an understanding of how lost we are without Him, the picture becomes complete. We need Jesus more than we need to breathe. He completes us. He gives purpose to our lives. And, conversely, without Jesus there's no hope, no future.

WHAT HAPPENED TO YOU?

When you step out to "do" evangelism, where do you start? How about beginning with you?

People want to know how you were changed. They want to know your story. They don't want you to tell them how to live. They do want you to give them advice based on the things you've struggled with. So, let's get started. We'd like to help you get your story together.

First, let's discuss your life before you met Christ. Make some notes below that describe what you were like.

_____

_____

_____

_____

_____

_____

Great. Now, let's get your conversion experience written down. It's okay if you don't have a specific experience. If you don't, write down how you felt immediately after you knew God had saved you. If you do have a specific experience, just write that down.

_____

_____

_____

_____

_____

_____

You're doing GREAT! Next we'd like you to write down what has changed in your life as a result of your relationship with Christ.

_____

_____

_____

_____

_____

_____

_____

_____

Finally, we'd like you to write down a few of the things that you've struggled with since you became a Christian.

_____

_____

_____

_____

_____

_____

Great job! Now, as we go through the following information, ask yourself these questions at the end of each section:

- How can I shape my story in such a way that others will hear what I am saying?
- What can I glean from where the current culture is heading that will help me be an effective evangelist?
- What aspect of evangelism is God calling me to? Homeless ministry? Pregnant unwed teens? Wall Street tycoons?

EVANGELISM IN THE NEW MILLENNIUM

Far Out!
A Far Side cartoon had the picture of a dog looking up at its owner with the owner vigorously scolding it.

WOW!

The owner was saying, "Sparky, I want you to eat all of the food in your bowl. I'm very disappointed in you for spilling some on the floor. You know Sparky that..."

Sparky heard, "Blah blah blah blah, Sparky. Blah, blah, blah, blah, blah, Sparky. Blah, blah, blah..."

Change. That's a huge word. The methods of evangelism must change. But what affects that change? How does society dictate that change? What's happening in the new millennium that hasn't happened in the past? Let's look at a variety of changes.

TRUTH 101

In the past, if you wanted to establish something as "true" to someone you were talking to, you gave them some sort of scientific description that proved it. Proving the validity of the Bible was easy because you had the Dead Sea Scrolls. Proving the existence of God became easier through some basic philosophical reasoning. But in the new millennium, proving the existence of anything will be done in an entirely different way. It'll be done through emotion. "I know this is true because it has affected me," and "This is true because I feel that it's true" will become ways to describe and prove the unseen.

TEACHER-LESS

Another interesting fact: Teaching has moved from didactic (I talk—you listen) to a more discussion-oriented format. Sure, people still want to hear things that are true from people who know something, but they want to be able to process and apply without someone telling them how.

Motherly Advice

Mother Teresa Says, "Do ordinary things with extraordinary love."

—Mother Teresa, *A Simple Path*, p. 99.

Kinda puts some perspective on how we can love others as we go about our daily lives, huh!

CATCH A CLUE

ANTI-CHRISTIAN

Postmoderns are highly anti-Christian. They love the concept of Jesus. In fact, they even revere Him. But because Christians are seen as dishonest, hateful, and ignorant, postmoderns are deterred from accepting the gospel.

GETTING THERE FIRST

Postmodern people recognize that God is at work in their lives long before they make the decision to be a disciple of Christ. They see that God's work in our lives is much more subtle and at the same time more dramatic than Christians give Him credit for. Therefore, postmodern evangelism is seen as something that helps people along in the process rather than inducting them in a new club. It seeks to help people know God, not adhere to a new set of rules.

An Expert Opinion

In his outstanding book *Jesus for a New Generation,* Kevin Graham Ford offers these ideas for the problems that face older people entering the new millennium. Ford goes on to offer ideas on how the gospel offers hope for the new millennium. (Ford, page 173)

- **People feel alienated.** The Christian story brings reconciliation. Ask yourself, "How can I bring reconciliation to this generation?" "What can I learn about the new trends facing the church that will help me reach them?"

- **People feel betrayed.** The Christian story brings promise and restores broken trust. The story also brings a sense of safety within a protective, healing community.
  Ask yourself, "How can God use me creatively to restore trust in this generation?" "How can I communicate the message of safety in Jesus so this generation will hear it?"

- **People are experiencing a lack of defined identity.** The Christian story gives them a new identity in Christ. They've been burned by a pathological model of authority. The Christian story reveals an authority that is positive, not pathological.

Ask yourself, "How can I demonstrate loving authority?" "How can I help people see Jesus as a caring figure of authority?"

• **People feel unwanted and unneeded**. The Christian story offers them a place of belonging, a place for involvement, a place where their lives can be used in service of a purpose that is larger than themselves.

Ask yourself, "How can I create an environment where people feel like they belong?" "What type of evangelism can we offer that spreads the message of Jesus and helps people feel like they fit in, no matter what their decision?"

EVANGELISM POST-ITS

A change in style can challenge even the most skilled evangelist. Once you're convinced that you need to change how you present the truth, there are things that are essential to remember. Here are a few:

Engage the Intellect

A new mentality means a new discovery of how things are thought about. Postmodern thought stays away from dogma and adheres to the discussion format. Through this format, the

THE BOTTOM LINE

Need Ideas?

Want the bottom line on where you can go to get up to date on the latest social issues to address?

- Watch TV. Especially the news or MTV. Look for stories where people are in conflict and consider how you can help.
- Read magazines that discuss social issues. Check out *Rolling Stone*, *Spin*, and *Wired* magazines.
- Talk a lot. People in your community probably have ideas about social concerns in your community. Also, your local newspaper just might have some clues too.

intellect is challenged, pushed, and stretched. The intellect is subject to more influences than before. Emotions weigh heavily on the intellect. They weigh in just as much as information. Engaging the intellect in a discussion or event that causes people to think is an effective beginning in evangelism.

Discuss Dogma—Don't Preach It

The new era of discussions is an era that cries to know the truth of the past, but not have it crammed down our throats. Discuss dogma. Feed the hunger to know and the hunger to discuss. Discuss moral codes. Wrestle with truth. But don't spoon-feed people the "right" answers. Instead, become an expert at asking leading questions. Get good at helping people understand truth instead of helping them learn how to creatively devour your beliefs.

Plain Talk

What words do you use to describe your walk with Christ? How would you tell people who have no exposure to God how you met Christ? Think about that for a moment. The truth is, how we describe our relationship with God to non-Christians says a lot about our heart for evangelism.

WIDE ANGLE

How to Do It

There are truths that traverse generations about why people need Jesus. Not convinced that you need to tell someone about your relationship with God? Consider these points that Paul Little points out in *How to Give Away Your Faith*.

- **Inner Emptiness.** Regardless of what generation they're from, many people feel a feeling of emptiness without God.
- **Purposelessness.** Another word to describe this might also be aimlessness. Without God many people feel like they're wandering in a forest and just can't find a way out.
- **Fear of Death.** While they might not admit it, many people are afraid of dying. Maybe it's the fear of the unknown. But without God, they've got no solid answers as to what happens after they die.
- **Desire for Inner Peace.** Emptiness. Purposelessness. Fearing death. All of these lead lost souls to a search for inner peace.
- **Loneliness.** Some people combat their loneliness by getting out and meeting people, getting involved in their communities, traveling, etc. But a large majority of people are lonely.

Consider dropping your "Christianease." Get it? Loose the language. Drop words like "washed in the blood" and "saved." Add phrases like "following Jesus" and "relationship with God."

Love First—Ask Questions Later

The single most powerful key for evangelism is love. Consider the fact that the push for loving others isn't a new concept. However, loving others is tougher these days. You've got to love people who don't believe what you believe, in the hopes of beginning a discussion about Jesus. Loving others in the new millennium means holding their hands and helping them understand the truth that you've found. Christians shouldn't use love to "hook" others and then bash them with the truth.

Think about others' eternal destiny. People are hopelessly lost without Jesus. Let their lostness motivate you to use whatever means you can think of to tell them how God has changed you.

PLACES TO "DO" EVANGELISM IN A NEW WAY

POOR, HOMELESS, BROKEN

No doubt, in your city there are people who need someone to rescue them. Consider reaching out to these people in the following ways.

THE BIBLE SAYS

Always Is a Long Time

"A friend loves at all times, and a brother is born for adversity."
—Proverbs 17:17

Open your church

There's probably space in your church. One tangible way to reach out to homeless people is to clear out some meeting rooms through the week and put cots and blankets out. Then put the word out in the community that, on certain nights, your church is open to homeless people.

Abused groups

Our society is littered with people who need someone to talk to—someone who could counsel them. However, for too long these people have found refuge in places other than the church. Consider the outreach that your church could have to broken people. When you open your doors to them, they could get ministered to in a nonthreatening environment. And, those who work with them would get ministered to as well.

Poverty

Poor people need help. This is another group of people who have found refuge mostly outside the boundaries of the church. Consider reaching these people by:

Establishing a money fund. You can't give handouts to everyone who knocks on the door of your church, but you can establish a base of money that can help truly needy people. Churches have long had funds that helped poorer people, but have done so with an attitude of reservation. Sometimes, being evangelistic means you have to substantially meet their physical needs before they'll hear about Jesus.

Helping them find a job. Teach them what to wear to an interview. Show them how to act. Help them create a resume.

Teaching them special skills. If they are unable to get a job, consider having training classes in your church. Teach them computer programs, child care, etc.

FORUMS

Discussions about Christianity will give way to the forum. Forums are:

Non-Christian discussions

Host articulate non-Christians to share why they don't believe in Christ. Use their points as discussion starters in breakout groups.

Truth Forums

Host several philosophy students or professors to lecture or lead discussions on what truth is, how truth is found, and what one does when they have discovered truth.

Apologetics Groups

Arrange groups to learn and apply the practice of apologetics.

GET SOCIAL

The onslaught of disenfranchised people is growing. The church stands in a strategic place to reach out to people whom society has forgotten—or people who are hurting and confused.

In all of these social issues, the church has an opportunity to be seen as people who love. Love even though. . . Love in spite of. . . Love even when. . . Now, how in the world can you evangelize through social action? First, giving demonstrates that we love people—an indispensable message that non-Christians need to see. Second, it gives non-Christians a place to serve before they discover Christ. In that environment of serving, awesome discussions about who Jesus is can take place.

Consider the following ministries as you step out to love.

Gays and Lesbians

These people stand in the gray area of society. Politicians use them either to bolster support or divide peoples. But these people need to be loved. Love them regardless of their belief about God. Love them into a belief about God.

Racial Reconciliation

The iron curtain has fallen on the White-Black-Hispanic-Asian issue—so why hasn't the church gotten more involved? Set yourself apart in your community as the church who seeks to reconcile the church to the minority groups in the city.

The Environment

You can care about the earth without worshiping it. These days, people are more concerned than ever about the quality of air that we breathe, the quality of water that we drink. They're concerned about the pollution, the ozone, and the various chemicals that we're manufacturing that create global problems. When you demonstrate that you care about the environment, you make your church look open to a group of people who really care about the condition of the earth.

WHERE TO GO

So, where can you go to tell people about Jesus? How close are you to the mission field?

Your Backyard

Consider making your neighborhood your target area. The people you see regularly as you're taking out the trash or washing your car might be the very people whom you can talk to about your relationship with Jesus.

- **Bible Clubs.** Host a summer Bible club. Host a neighborhood small group. Make your church open to non-Christians by first making your home open.
- **Neighborhood Service.** Here's an idea—put your barbecue on your front porch and give hamburgers away to your neighbors. You'll open a

door to talk with them, and you'll serve them at the same time.

Your Work

If you're like most of the population of the U.S., you probably have some contact with people through work. Use this arena to build relationships and demonstrate the love of God.

• **Talk Openly.** Refer to your walk with Christ often. Identify yourself with Christianity. But be careful to follow up everything you say with actions.

Around the Church

Those who live around your church see a side of you that you might not expect. They see how you treat your kids before and after you've been in God's presence. They watch how well you keep up your property.

But they're also watching in hopes that you'll do something they can be a part of. They want to be involved, but they're skeptical. Consider going after these people as a start to your evangelism.

Being a Friend

Millennials have established a majority of their friendships via the Internet. They are craving human touch outside of cyberspace. Christians have an incredible opportunity to reach out to this generation simply by being their friend.

SECTION 7

THE END TIMES?

END TIMES MANIA

Remember how popular the *Thief in the Night* movies were in the 1970s? Or have you browsed through a Christian bookstore lately and found dozens of books on the end times? It's not difficult to see why there has been an end times fervor in the last century.

- Israel was founded and survived enemy attacks.
- Russia, the Evil Empire, was the enemy.
- Saddam Hussein, the favorite antichrist of the 1990s ruled Iraq (ancient Babylon).
- The United Nations moved us toward a one-world government.
- The occult became popular once again.

These changes to the world, coupled with emphatic preaching, made it seem as if the end of the world was near. In addition to the above changes there were many events that the Bible seems to forecast as evidence of the end times. Matthew 24 says that during the end times, the world will be full of:

- Wars and rumors of wars
- Famines
- Earthquakes
- Christians being persecuted
- Evil
- The gospel being preached throughout the world

- False signs and false christs who will arise and trick many people
- Less love

In addition to the above list, 2 Timothy 3:1–5 adds this:
"There will be terrible times in the last days. People will be:
- lovers of themselves,
- lovers of money,
- boastful,
- proud,
- abusive,
- disobedient to their parents,
- ungrateful,
- unholy,
- without love,
- unforgiving,
- slanderous,
- without self-control,
- brutal,
- not lovers of the good,
- treacherous,
- rash,
- conceited,
- lovers of pleasure rather than lovers of God—
- having a form of godliness but denying its power."

A scan down these two lists makes it seem like we're living in the end times and Jesus might be ready to arrive in the next twenty-four hours. Right?

Maybe—but maybe not.

LIFE'S BEEN THIS BAD BEFORE

It's a well-circulated urban legend that society is growing more evil than ever before. Christians ask, "How much more will God be willing to take?"

Compared to certain eras of American history, those observations ring true. But compared to the global world history, many argue that we're not any more or any less evil than before. For example, is today's society worse than the era of the Roman empire when violence and murder was everywhere; infanticide was practiced; temple prostitutes were the norm; and people fighting animals to the death in the coliseum was *entertainment?* We complain that our movies are too violent, but back then the blood that flowed was real.

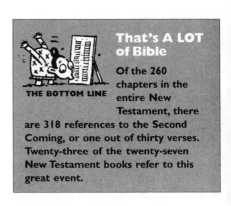

THE BOTTOM LINE

That's A LOT of Bible

Of the 260 chapters in the entire New Testament, there are 318 references to the Second Coming, or one out of thirty verses. Twenty-three of the twenty-seven New Testament books refer to this great event.

Both societies were made of good and bad. The same can be said about almost any era of human history. To remember one time period as better might be more due to wishful thinking and nostalgia than truth.

BUT PEOPLE HAVE BEEN TALKING

There's been a lot of discussion about the end times of late. Many books have been written about it, many preachers have preached about it, and many Christians have speculated, *It must be near.*

It might be true and few Christians would object to putting aside their

earthly existence for a heavenly one. But these discussions and specula-
tions aren't new. *Lots* of people over the years have thought and taught
that Jesus' return was right around the corner. Check out some well-known
examples:

A.D. *381*
Tyconius, a leader in the church, taught that Jesus would
return in 381. He didn't.

A.D. *1260*
Joachim of Fiore (1135–1202) convinced many that Jesus
would return in 1260. Still no Jesus.

A.D. *1533*
Melchior Hoffmann, a radical reformer in Germany, taught
that Jesus would return in 1533. Nope, not yet.

A.D. *1843*
A New England preacher, William Miller, taught widely
that Jesus would return in 1843. Over fifty thousand
Christians believed and were disappointed.

A.D. *1914*
Charles Russell, founder of the Jehovah's Witnesses,
predicted Jesus would return in 1914. Jehovah's Witnesses
believe that He did come back in spirit but would become
visible in 1975—uh, oh, missed that one, too.

A.D. *1981*
Hal Lindsay, author of the *Late Great Planet Earth*, pre-

dicted that the rapture of Christians would occur in 1981. We *still* here?

September 11-13, 1988
A Christian book titled *88 Reasons Why the Rapture Is in 1988* was published. After Jesus didn't return, the same author released a book *89 Reasons Why the Rapture is in 1989.* (If at first you don't succeed, try...)

October 28, 1992
A full-page advertisement appeared in *USA Today* in 1991 alerting the world that Jesus would return in October of 1992. Oops.

September 1994
Harold Camping, president of Family Radio, wrote a book entitled *1994?* This book predicted that Jesus would return in September 1994.

A.D. 1996
Many prophecy teachers announced that 1996 (2000 years from Christ's birth in 4 B.C.) would be the year.

March 31, 1998
A Taiwanese sect believed that Jesus would return and be seen by the whole world—on channel 18 of your local TV. (Talk about your "Must See TV"!)

WHAT'S THE POINT?

In one sense, these failed predictions aren't all bad. The Bible teaches about the end times and Jesus' second coming for a number of reasons.

- We're supposed to look forward to Jesus coming.
- We're supposed to live a holy life as if Jesus were coming back today.
- We're supposed to live with our hearts beating for heaven.
- We're supposed to live with a loose grasp on our earthly success and possessions.
- We're supposed to tell others about Jesus as if He were coming back soon.

The problem arises, though, when we focus on the Rapture or the Antichrist and not on Christ. If Christians knew, loved, and focused on Christ, we'd already do

DON'T FORGET

Need a Lift?

Evangelist Billy Graham once said: "One of the best ways to get rid of discouragement is to remember that Christ is coming again. The most thrilling, glorious truth in all the world is the Second Coming of Jesus Christ.

"When we look around and see pessimism on every side, we should remember the Bible is the only Book in the world that predicts the future. The Bible is more modern than tomorrow morning's newspaper.

"The Bible accurately foretells the future, and it says that the consummation of all things shall be the coming again of Jesus Christ to this earth.

"If your life is dismal, depressed, and gloomy today, Christ can turn those dark clouds inside out. The sunlight of His love can still shine into the darkest part of your life."

the things on the above list. Our goal should be to love Christ and do the work He's given us to do. When we do, we'll find ourselves fulfilling that list pretty well.

WHY PICKING DATES IS BAD

Reminding people to live like Jesus is about to return is good. Predicting dates for Jesus' return is not. Failed predictions are bad for many reasons:

Predicting dates makes Christians the butt of jokes.

In the 1990s there were many cults in the news that believed some strange things. David Koresh's group in Waco, Texas thought the world was about to end in a great firestorm. The Heaven's Gate cult believed that a UFO was arriving behind a comet and would take them to a new life. A Taiwanese cult announced that Jesus was going to return on March 31, 1998 on channel 18. It's easy to understand why all these groups were poked fun at in the media and around the water coolers of America. When well-meaning Christians stand up and make predictions that remain unfulfilled, the

WOW!

Nine Antichrists

The magazine *Christian History* has compiled a list of nine people who have been labeled the Antichrist.

Nero (d. 68): "He will descend from his firmament in the form of a man, a king of iniquity, a murderer of his mother—this is the king of this world. . . . He will act and speak like the Beloved, and will say, 'I am the Lord, and before me there was no one.' "
—*Martyrdom of Isaiah* (late first-century apocalyptic text)

Justinian (d. 565): "Many men have been born who. . .have shown themselves terrible beings. But to destroy all men and to ruin the whole earth has been granted to none save. . .Justinian, Prince of demons."
—*Procopius, Secret History* (late sixth-century)

Hitler (d. 1945): "I believe today that I am acting in the sense of the Almighty Creator. By warding off the Jews, I am fighting for the Lord's work."
—Adolf Hitler, *Mein Kampf*

Frederick II (d. 1250): "What other Antichrist should we await, when as is evident in his works, he is already come in the person of Frederick? He is the author of every crime, stained by every cruelty, and he has invaded the patrimony of Christ seeking to destroy it with Saracen aid."
—Pope Gregory IX

Napoleon (d. 1821): A friend of Samuel Johnson's " . . .was always happy to cite evidence of [the French Revolution's] Antichrist-like character, culminating in Napoleon, whose name she believed meant 'the Destroyer.' "
—Historian Bernard McGinn, *Antichrist*

Reagan: "The beast recovers from a mortal wound, which, in the 1980s, caused quite a stir in evangelical circles when Ronald Wilson Reagan—each name having six letters—was shot and yet survived."
—*Robert Fuller*

Naming the Antichrist:

Gorbachev: Gorbachev! Has the Real Antichrist Come?
—Title of a 1988 book by Robert Faird

Luther (d. 1546): "He has rejected the sacraments, repudiated the expunging of sins through fasts, and rejects the daily celebration of the Mass. . . . Does this sound to you like Christ or Antichrist?"
—Pope Hadrian VI

John Paul II: "[This man] will be increasingly called upon to bring peace to a troubled world. His recovery from a deadly wound directed world attention and admiration to his personage, and he, like those before him, would seemingly like to establish authority over the Holy Hill of Zion."
—Radio host Noah Hutchings

results are the same.

But Christians are supposed to be persecuted, some would say. *So what if the world laughs. The Bible says that Christians are going to be persecuted anyway. It just comes with the territory, right?* Wrong.

Jesus said that we'd be persecuted for our belief in Him and for the sake of the gospel. Making foolish predictions about Jesus' return, then accepting ridicule probably prepares someone more for the Hall of Folly rather than the Hall of Sainthood.

WOW!

Great Timing

The Reverend Earl Kelly, pastor of the First Baptist Church of Holly Springs, Mississippi, was preaching on the Second Coming of Christ.

He had just quoted Matthew 24:27, *"For as the lightning cometh out of the east, and shineth even unto the west; so shall also the coming of the Son of man be" (KJV).*

At this point, a large lightbulb fell from its socket in the ceiling and shattered on the floor in front of the pulpit.

As reported by *Baptist Press,* Kelly was equal to the occasion. He told the startled worshippers, "His coming will be just as sudden, and unexpected, and devastating to the dreams that are not Christ-centered."
—*Christianity Today*

Predicting dates makes Christianity seem less credible.

Christians should have a lot of credibility. The Bible teaches *many* things that are absolute, concrete, and true. We take away credibility from those things when we tell people that the Bible says Jesus is going to return next July 4 in a cloud of fireworks.

Predicting dates causes Christians to grow discouraged.

Imagine yourself as a child. Imagine that your parents tell you that at Christmas you're going to get the toy you've always wanted—an electric train. You eagerly wake up Christmas day and unwrap all your presents but find no train. Your father casually tells you that you'll get the train next year. You wait a year and relive your excitement again—but again, no train. He promises you next year. . .

By predicting dates, we do the same thing to fellow Christians. We promise something that we cannot give and the result is disheartening.

BUT HE IS COMING

But Jesus is coming—is that bad to talk about? No. But we should stick to what we *know*. We know Christ is coming, we know He's going to judge the world, we know that Christians will live forever with Him in heaven, but we don't know when.

We Predict: More Predictions Coming

Predictions haven't ended. The beginning of the new millennium will have a number of new predictions. Keep in mind that the best advice for Christians is the old adage, "Live like Christ was coming back today, but plan on Christ coming back in 100 years."

WHAT DOES THE BIBLE SAY ABOUT THE END OF THE WORLD?

The world will end one day. While the Bible doesn't give dates, times, or names, it does make it clear that the end will come. Here are the signs that the Bible gives of the end times (taken from the *End Times Bible*, published by World Publishing):

Sign	*Reference*
People living as if God didn't exist	Genesis 6:5; Luke 17:26
Vacuum in world leadership	Psalm 2:1–3; Revelation 13:4-9
Explosion of knowledge and freedom of travel	Daniel 12:4
Wars and rumors of wars	Mark 13:7
Widespread acceptance of immoral behavior	Luke 17:26-30; 2 Peter 2:1–8
Human leader declares himself to be God	2 Thessalonians 2:3–4
Increased demonic activity	1 Timothy 4:1–3
Widespread abandonment of the Christian faith	1 Timothy 4:1; 2 Timothy 4:3–4
Evidence of breakdown in families	2 Timothy 3:1–3
Spirit of selfishness and materialism	2 Timothy 3:1–2
General disrespect for others	2 Timothy 3:2–4
People ridiculing God's Word	2 Peter 3:2-4; Jude 17–18
Significant shifts in political power and influence	Revelation 13:3–7

THE ANTICHRIST

In addition to the changes in the world, a leader the Bible calls the Antichrist will arise. Many Christians believe that the Antichrist will disgrace the temple in Jerusalem and then begin a period of tribulation, which will end when Christ returns. Other Christians believe that the Antichrist already disgraced and destroyed the temple in A.D. 70 and that we're now living in a state of tribulation, which will end when Christ returns.

THE RAPTURE, TRIBULATION, AND OTHER STUFF

There are lots of views about the end times, how they will occur, and what will happen. Here's a chart used by permission from the *End Times Bible* that helps define the four major views.

Dispensational Premillennialism	*Historic Premillennialism*	*Amillennialism*	*Postmillennialism*
The Rapture	**The Rapture**	**The Rapture**	**The Rapture**
The church is raptured prior to the tribulation and taken to heaven to be with Christ.	The rapture is part of the Second Coming—when believers join Christ in the air to descend to earth with Him.	The rapture is part of the Second Coming—when believers join Christ in the air to descend to earth with Him.	The rapture is part of the Second Coming—when believers join Christ in the air to descend to earth with Him.

Dispensational Premillennialism	*Historic Premillennialism*	*Amillennialism*	*Postmillennialism*
The Antichrist	**The Antichrist**	**The Antichrist**	**The Antichrist**
The Antichrist is a person who will appear during the end times to personify satanic power. He will make a treaty with Israel and then persecute that nation.	The antichrist is a person who will appear during the end times to personify satanic power.	The antichrist represents satanic power throughout this age. Perhaps a person, personifying satanic power at the end of our age, will appear.	The antichrist represents satanic power throughout the church age. Most biblical references to the antichrist have already been fulfilled.
Tribulation	**Tribulation**	**Tribulation**	**Tribulation**
The church is raptured to heaven before the tribulation. Israel is converted through the tribulation.	The church goes through the tribulation.	The church goes through the tribulation, which is a final outbreak of evil at the end of this age.	The tribulation is this present age. Evil lessens towards the end of this age.
Second Coming	**Second Coming**	**Second Coming**	**Second Coming**
The Second Coming will occur in two phases. First, the church will be raptured. Seven years later, Christ will return to earth to establish the millennium.	Jesus' Second Coming will establish the millennium.	Jesus' Second Coming will establish the new heaven and new earth.	Jesus' Second Coming after the millennium will establish the new heaven and new earth.

Dispensational Premillennialism	Historic Premillennialism	Amillennialism	Postmillennialism
Resurrection	**Resurrection**	**Resurrection**	**Resurrection**
The resurrection will occur in three phases: (1) dead believers at the rapture, (2) Old Testament saints at Jesus' Second Coming, and (3) the remaining dead at the end of the millennium.	The resurrection will occur in two phases: (1) the resurrection of all dead believers at Jesus' Second Coming, and (2) the resurrection of the remaining dead at the end of the millennium.	One general resurrection of believing and unbelieving dead will occur at the Second Coming.	One general resurrection of believing and unbelieving dead will occur at the Second Coming.
Judgment	**Judgment**	**Judgment**	**Judgment**
Judgment will occur in three phases. (1) At the rapture, believers will be judged. (2) At the Second Coming, the living Jews will be judged (3) At the end of the millennium, unbelievers will be judged.	Judgment will occur in two phases. (1) At the Second Coming, believers' works will be judged. (2) At the end of the millennium, everyone will face the final judgment.	At the Second Coming, all people will be judged.	At the Second Coming, occurring at the end of the millennium, there will be one judgment of all people.

Dispensational Premillennialism	Historic Premillennialism	Amillennialism	Postmillennialism
Millennium	Millennium	Millennium	Millennium
The millennium is a thousand-year period that fulfills Old Testament promises for the nation of Israel. Jesus reigns literally in Jerusalem. The curse is removed from the earth. The church is in heaven.	Jesus reigns visibly on earth. The millennium is for both Old Testament and New Testament believers. The curse is removed from the earth.	Jesus reigns now in the hearts of believers and through the church. There is no future literal millennium on earth. This age ends with the Second Coming.	Jesus is leading the church in this present age to preach the Good News throughout the world. This preaching of the Good News will establish the millennium on earth.

WHAT SHOULD WE GET OUT OF THIS?

Well, if we can't know exactly *when* Christ will return and Christians are not agreed on *how* He will return, what's the point of thinking about it at all?

It reminds us that Earth is not our final home
Earth is the place we'll live for a short period of time—one hundred years maybe. After our years have ended, we'll spend an eternity in the afterlife. Christians will spend that time in God's presence in heaven. The Bible holds up Abraham and other great people of the Bible who remain good

models for us: "They admitted that they were aliens and strangers on earth. . . . Instead, they were longing for a better country—a heavenly one" (Hebrews 11:13, 16).

It reminds us to live right

Second Peter 3:11, in talking about the end of the world says, "Since everything will be destroyed in this way, what kind of people ought you to be? You ought to live holy and godly lives." Hearing about the end times and the new millennium should remind us to please God by how we live.

It reminds us to tell others about God

We shouldn't use scare tactics to scare people into Christianity. If their

WOW!

The Queen Knew Her Place

"Many are the stories which tell of that beautiful world-famed Queen Victoria, but this appealed to me almost as none other that I ever heard.

"One day as she listened to the chaplain preach a sermon on the significance of the coming again of Jesus to the world, those near the royal box noticed the beautiful queen as she shook with emotion, as her lips quivered, and as her eyes were suffused with tears.

"When the service was ended she asked to see the chaplain alone, and when he was ushered into her presence and beheld her great emotion, he asked her its occasion, and she said, 'Oh, sir, it was what you said about the coming again of the world's rightful King.'

"And he said, 'Why are you so moved?'

"Queen Victoria said, 'I could wish to be here when He comes!' And then, with emotion indescribable and sublimely glorious, she said, 'that I might lay this crown at His blessed feet.'" —Dr. George W. Truett faith is based on fear, they'll have no reason to stay once their fears are alleviated. But Christ's future return should motivate us to tell others the gospel message.

SECTION 8
YOUR PERSONAL FUTURE

THREE-WAY THINKING

HOW SHOULD YOU MAKE YOUR PLANS FOR THE FUTURE?

Making plans for the future? Good for you. Preparedness is an admirable quality. But unless you've read the following descriptions of how we should be planning for the days ahead, you really aren't prepared. Do yourself a favor: Read on.

WITH AN EYE ON THE PAST

It was George Santayana who said, "Those who cannot remember the past are condemned to repeat it." These words are especially relevant when it comes to our personal histories. If we do not learn from the mistakes we've made in the past, we're doomed to keep making them over and over again.

By the same token, we must also keep in mind the triumphs and highlights of our past, with an eye toward repeating those actions or duplicating those circumstances in the future.

There's a big difference, of course, between keeping an eye on the past and living in it. What's done is done. Barring some new development in time travel technology, nothing about our pasts can be changed. Obsessing over events of years gone by is pointless and counterproductive.

WITH AN EYE ON WHAT'S REALLY IMPORTANT

When you think about the future, what areas do you tend to concentrate on? Chances are, you've spent more than a little time wondering about how much money you'll have, what kind of house you'll own, what kind of car you'll drive, what kind of clothes you'll wear, and so on. Sometimes it's fun to think about those things. Usually, though, it's a waste of time.

You see, in God's way of looking at the future, possessions are mere afterthoughts. What's really important is that we keep our priorities straight. In Matthew 22:37–39, Jesus sums it up this

THE BIBLE SAYS

Most Important

"I denied myself nothing my eyes desired; I refused my heart no pleasure. My heart took delight in all my work, and this was the reward for all my labor. Yet when I surveyed all that my hands had done and what I had toiled to achieve, everything was meaningless, a chasing after the wind; nothing was gained under the sun." (Ecclesiastes 2:10-11)

"Oh, for the days when I was in my prime, when God's intimate friendship blessed my house, when the Almighty was still with me and my children were around me, when my path was drenched with cream and the rock poured out for me streams of olive oil." (Job 29:4-6)

way: " 'Love the Lord your God with all your heart and with all your soul and with all your mind.' This is the first and greatest commandment. And the second is like it: 'Love your neighbor as yourself.' " These three short verses should set the tone for our future plans. If the Lord does not figure heavily into your agenda, it's time to make a new one.

WITH AN EYE ON GOD'S WILL

You've got three choices when it comes to your future. One, you can do your own thing, without giving a second thought to God or His will. Two, you can do your own thing, hoping that your choices will coincide with God's will. Or, three, you can seek out God's will before making your decisions.

May we recommend option number three? The thing is, when it's your way against God's way, your way doesn't stand a chance. You cannot outthink God. You may think you know what's best for you, but you don't. You're only living your life; God created it. He knows exactly what you were meant to do and what it will take for you to achieve ultimate satisfaction and peace in your life. Think about what the Bible says:

THE BIBLE SAYS

First Things First

"Then Jesus said to his disciples: 'Therefore I tell you, do not worry about your life, what you will eat; or about your body, what you will wear. Life is more than food, and the body more than clothes. Consider the ravens: They do not sow or reap, they have no storeroom or barn; yet God feeds them. And how much more valuable you are than birds! Who of you by worrying can add a single hour to his life? Since you cannot do this very little thing, why do you worry about the rest?' "
—Luke 12:22-26

"But seek first his kingdom and his righteousness, and all these things will be given to you as well. Therefore do not worry about tomorrow, for tomorrow will worry about itself. Each day has enough trouble of its own."
—Matthew 6:33

"To man belong the plans of the heart, but from the LORD comes the reply of the tongue. All a man's ways seem innocent to him, but motives are weighed by the LORD. Commit to the LORD whatever you do, and your plans will succeed.

"The LORD works out everything for his own ends—even the wicked for a day of disaster. The LORD detests all the proud of heart. Be sure of this: They will not go unpunished. Through love and faithfulness sin is atoned for; through the fear of the LORD a man avoids evil. When a man's ways are pleasing to the LORD, he makes even his enemies live at peace with him. Better a little with righteousness than much gain with injustice. In his heart a man plans his course, but the LORD determines his steps." (Proverbs 16:1–9)

And,

"Be very careful, then, how you live—not as unwise but as wise, making the most of every opportunity, because the days are evil. Therefore do not be foolish, but understand what the Lord's will is." (Ephesians 5:15–17)

CERTAINTIES

WHAT DO WE KNOW FOR SURE ABOUT THE FUTURE?

For the most part, the future is a mystery that cannot be solved, only guessed at. Being three-dimensional creatures, humans have no way to see beyond the realm of our current existence. We can make educated guesses as to what the future holds in certain areas, but for the most part the future is unknowable—with a few significant exceptions. Below you'll find three absolutes concerning the future, three islands of permanence in a vast sea of uncertainty.

God is sovereign.

The world has seen its share of powerful leaders—Genghis Khan,

God's in Charge

"Yours, O LORD, is the greatness and the power and the glory and the majesty and the splendor, for everything in heaven and earth is yours. Yours, O LORD, is the kingdom; you are exalted as head over all. Wealth and honor come from you; you are the ruler of all things. In your hands are strength and power to exalt and give strength to all. Now, our God, we give you thanks, and praise your glorious name."
(I Chronicles 29:11-13)

"The LORD reigns forever; he has established his throne for judgment. He will judge the world in righteousness; he will govern the peoples with justice."
(Psalm 9:7-8)

"Now to the King eternal, immortal, invisible, the only God, be honor and glory for ever and ever. Amen."
(I Timothy 1:17)

Alexander the Great, Darth Vader (just seeing if you're awake). Compared to the sovereignty of God, though, these leaders' reigns seem puny and insignificant. After all, the best a human leader can hope for is to rule over land and people. God, on the hand, reigns supreme not only over the physical world, but over time and space itself.

Nothing in the world has happened, can happen, or will happen without God allowing it to. Nothing is a mystery to Him. He's not only seen everything that's happened in the past, He's seen everything that's going to happen in the future. Time can do nothing to lessen His sovereignty.

Comfort and direction is available.

No one can guarantee you a pain-free future. No one can guarantee that the path you'll travel will be smooth and clearly marked. Chances are, you'll experience your fair share of hardships and directionless moments. People you depend on for support, companionship, and wisdom will drop out of your life. Choices that once seemed clear and obvious will turn out to be mistakes. The future can be a scary place.

Fortunately for us, the Lord "is the same yesterday, today and forever" (Hebrews 13:8). Just as He is available to us today, He will be available tomorrow and for the rest of our lives. Comfort, direction, and assurance will always be just a prayer away. Consider these verses:

> "The LORD is a refuge for the oppressed, a stronghold in times of trouble. Those who know your name will trust in you, for you, LORD, have never forsaken those who seek you." (Psalm 9:9-10)

And,

"If any of you lacks wisdom, he should ask God, who gives generously to all without finding fault, and it will be given to him. But when he asks, he must believe and not doubt, because he who doubts is like a wave of the sea, blown and tossed by the wind." (James 1:5-6)

Heaven awaits those who trust in the Lord.

Will you be married twenty years from now? How many kids will you have? Where will you be working? Where will you be living? Will you be living? If so, what will your life be like? What will you be like? What will you look like? How many of the people you know now will still be a part of your life? These are all good questions, but they're unanswerable.

If you'd care to move your focus beyond the short-term future, though, the picture becomes considerably clearer. In fact, if you're a Christian, you can confidently predict where you'll be a thousand years from now. All believers are promised eternal life with God Himself in heaven. We may live in a temporary world now, but God has designed us with a yearning for something permanent, something eternal. We may not understand it. We may not even recognize that it's there. But it is. And it's a yearning that will be fulfilled.

There are a lot of challenges in this world, a lot of hurt, a lot of grief, a lot of pressure, and a lot of uncertainty. When it all gets to be too much, think about what lies ahead—your very own heavenly mansion, designed especially for you by Jesus Himself.

THE BIBLE SAYS

Trust God for Your Future

"He has made everything beautiful in its time. He has also set eternity in the hearts of men; yet they cannot fathom what God has done from beginning to end." (Ecclesiastes 3:11)

"Do not let your hearts be troubled. Trust in God; trust also in me. In my Father's house are many rooms; if it were not so, I would have told you. I am going there to prepare a place for you. And if I go and prepare a place for you, I will come back and take you to be with me that you also may be where I am. You know the way to the place where I am going. (John 14:1-4)

"Now we know that if the earthly tent we live in is destroyed, we have a building from God, an eternal house in heaven, not built by human hands. Meanwhile we groan, longing to be clothed with our heavenly dwelling, because when we are clothed, we will not be found naked. For while we are in this tent, we groan and are burdened, because we do not wish to be unclothed but to be clothed with our heavenly dwelling, so that what is mortal may be swallowed up by life. Now it is God who has made us for this very purpose and has given us the Spirit as a deposit, guaranteeing what is to come." (2 Corinthians 5:1-5)

A PLACE IN THIS WORLD

REALIZING YOUR LIFE'S MISSION

Help When You Need It

"Humble yourselves, therefore, under God's mighty hand, that he may lift you up in due time. Cast all your anxiety on him because he cares for you." (I Peter 5:6-7)

THE BIBLE SAYS

Do you ever feel like a jigsaw puzzle piece that was put in the wrong box? Does it ever seem to you that there's just no place in this world where you fit in? Well, then join the rest of us odd puzzle pieces. We all feel out of place at one time or another. The key is to look beyond our times of displacement toward the future plan that God has in store for us. He does have a plan for your life, and He will reveal it you—when He's ready. In the meantime, here are some things you can do to prepare for your life's mission.

Pray.

In college, if you're facing a big test, it's always wise to talk to the professor about it. After all, he's the one who created the exam, so he knows everything that's on it. You could ask him to tell you all of the answers, but that would be cheating. Besides, you'd never learn anything if all the answers were just given to you. A better strategy would be to ask your professor what you need to know in order to do well on the test. Even the smallest hints here and there will make a world of difference in the final outcome of the exam.

The same principles hold true with seeking our life's mission. The wisest thing we can do is talk to God about it. After all, He's the one who created us, so He knows everything about us. You could ask Him to tell you everything that the future holds for you, but that would be a mistake. You'd miss the many opportunities for discovering things about yourself and about God that go along with the search for one's purpose in life. A better strategy would be to ask God to reveal enough about your life's mission to start you off on the right track. Even the smallest hints here and there will make a world of difference as you boldly explore your future.

Your Role

"Just as each of us has one body with many members, and these members do not all have the same function, so in Christ we who are many form one body, and each member belongs to all the others. We have different gifts, according to the grace given us. If a man's gift is prophesying, let him use it in proportion to his faith. If it is serving, let him serve; if it is teaching, let him teach; if it is encouraging, let him encourage; if it is contributing to the needs of others, let him give generously; if it is leadership, let him govern diligently; if it is showing mercy, let him do it cheerfully." (Romans 12:4-8)

THE BIBLE SAYS

Explore your gifts.

God didn't hand out our natural talents, skills, and abilities randomly, like a clown handing out balloons on a parade route. He had a reason for giving us the gifts we possess. Chances are, our gifts will figure heavily in our life's mission. Perhaps the best thing we can do to discover God's plan for our future is to use the talents and abilities He's given us today. If we keep our eyes peeled while we put our skills to use, we may just get a glimpse of what lies ahead for us.

Seek advice from the right people.

Wise acquaintances may be the most valuable assets anyone can have. Find some people who know you well, whether it be your parents, your spouse, your kids, your boss, your pastor, your Sunday school teacher, or any

other mature Christian whose opinion you trust. Talk with them about your search for your life's mission. Get their opinions as to the skills and talents they think you should pursue. You may be surprised to find out that others see abilities in you that you've never noticed before.

Pray again.

That's right, we're recommending that you pray again. (In fact, we recommend that you pray as often as possible as you search for your life's mission.) After you've explored your gifts and talked to

Get Help!

"Plans fail for lack of counsel, but with many advisers they succeed."
(Proverbs 15:22)

THE BIBLE SAYS

"Ask and it will be given to you; seek and you will find; knock and the door will be opened to you. For everyone who asks receives; he who seeks finds; and to him who knocks, the door will be opened."
(Matthew 7:7-8)

people you trust about your decision, ask the Lord to help you sort through the information you gathered. Ask Him to help you decide which advice to pay attention to and which to ignore. Ask Him to make your next step clear to you, to open the next "door" that He'd like you to enter. Finally, ask Him to give you peace about His plan when He finally reveals it to you.

Get in gear.

Eventually God will open your eyes to His plan for your life. He will also lead you to the place where you can put that plan into action. When He does, you need to act swiftly and decisively. If there's a decision to be made and you feel God's leading, don't hem and haw. Be a doer, not just a listener.

THE BIBLE SAYS

As for the Bible

"Do not merely listen to the word, and so deceive yourselves. Do what it says. Anyone who listens to the word but does not do what it says is like a man who looks at his face in a mirror and, after looking at himself, goes away and immediately forgets what he looks like. But the man who looks intently into the perfect law that gives freedom, and continues to do this, not forgetting what he has heard, but doing it—he will be blessed in what he does." (James 1:22-25)

THE ONES THAT REALLY MATTER

MAKING BIG DECISIONS

Many of the choices we make every day don't require much thought. Some decisions are screamingly obvious. Others involve such minor consequences that it matters little whether the right choice is made or not. And then there are the "biggies," the decisions that carry with them enormous consequences. These are the ones that require a plan of action. This is the place to find such a plan. Below we've listed five important tips for making the right decision when the stakes are high.

Engage in some vertical conversations.

You didn't think we'd suggest anything but prayer as your first order of business, did you? If you're facing a big decision regarding your future, who better to talk to than the One who holds the future? Ask the Lord to clear your mind of the worries, pressures, and other things that may be clouding your vision. Ask Him to give you a sense of peace and a sense of direction— the peace for your mental health and the direction to help you know where to start in your decision-making process.

The Lord is gracious and faithful to those who love Him. What's more, He's always on the job, ready to step in and lend a hand anytime He's asked to. He will open the doors that He wants you to pass through and close those that lead to places you shouldn't be.

Be warned, though: To pray for the Lord's leading is to give up control of the situation to Him. If you want Him to guide your decision making, He will—in His own way.

Consult your family.

If you're facing a big decision in your life, chances are it will affect your loved ones as well. That being the case, you should make sure to give your friends and family members ample opportunity to weigh in on the topic. It's only fair, you know. Their opinions and preferences should be as important to you as your own are.

An obvious example would be a move. Let's say you've been offered a position at a firm several hundred miles from where you currently live. All of your kids are in school and your spouse has a decent-paying job at a nearby bank. For you, this is the chance of a lifetime: a high-profile, high-paying position at one of the leading companies in your industry. (We're talking college fund kind of money here.) Your spouse is excited for you, but is reluctant to move because of family obligations (an elderly parent) in the area. Your oldest daughter cries herself to sleep every night at the thought of leaving her friends and family. Your youngest daughter wants to move, but only because it means she'll get her own bedroom.

How eager would you be to get input from your family concerning the move? Whose opinion(s) would you seriously consider? Why? What kinds of things might persuade you one way or the other?

We're not suggesting that your life be dictated by the whims of those who live in your house. Sometimes difficult decisions have to be made, regardless of how unpleasant they may be. What we are suggesting is that you give your loved ones plenty of opportunities to voice their opinions on matters that will affect their lives.

Investigate.

Not all once-in-a-lifetime opportunities are what they seem. If you're poised to make a big decision, you owe it to yourself to make sure that you've gathered all of the relevant information you can get your hands on.

Continuing our earlier example of a move, you'll find that there are countless details you'll need to investigate before you decide whether to uproot your family or not. For example, what's the job market like in your new area? What's the community like? How different is it from the places your family has lived before? What economic trends should you be aware of? The list of possible questions is endless.

Consult experts—or at least some fairly intelligent people.

Don't try to make big-time life decisions on your own. In addition to seeking the opinion of your family members, you should also talk to some people who have relevant experience with the decision you're facing.

If it's a move that you're considering, talk to some people who have moved to your area recently. Find out what moving companies they used and what realtors they worked with. What kind of fees did they pay? What kind of service did they get? Take note of any strong recommendations or warnings. Use your Internet prowess to connect with people in the region where you're considering making your new home. Get some eyewitness accounts of what it's like to live there and what goes on in the way of entertainment or excitement.

Ultimately, the decision is yours. But remember: It doesn't hurt anything to pick the brains of people whose experience can help you make the best decision possible for you and your family.

Pull the trigger.

The most difficult aspect of the decision-making process is reaching that final conclusion. Regardless of how overwhelming the evidence is in your favor, there's always a flash of doubt when it comes time to seal the deal. Don't let that doubt discourage you. If you've presented your situation to the Lord in prayer and sought the advice of your family, friends, and other people whose opinions you trust, it's time to make your decision.

As a final note, we suggest that once you commit to the decision, you should not look back. There will likely be times when you'll be tempted to question the wisdom of your choice. Resist that temptation. Remind yourself that "in all things God works for the good of those who love him, who have been called according to his purpose" (Romans 8:28).

YOU AND YOUR JOB

ARE YOU ON THE RIGHT CAREER TRACK?

Even if you waited until after college to start your career and then retire early—say, at age fifty-five—you still have thirty-four years of work to look forward to. Assuming the bare-minimum forty-hour work week, you're still looking at over 65,000 hours on the job. That's a long time to spend doing anything. It's an eternity to spend doing something you don't like.

How can you know if the career you've chosen is the right one for your future? Here are a few questions you need to answer.

HOW DO YOU VIEW YOUR WORK?

It's morning. The alarm clock is sounding. What do you do?

- Do you leap out of bed, greet the new day with a broad grin, and hurriedly prepare yourself for another exciting day at the office? Do you whistle a happy tune on the way to work, butterflies fluttering in your stomach, overcome by the sheer excitement of the workday that lies before you? Do you waltz into your place of employment with a kind word and a hearty laugh for everyone you meet?

OR

• Do you hit the snooze bar five or six times, stumble out of bed with an exasperated groan, and knock back cup after cup of java in a futile effort to gather your wits about you? Do you mutter and curse at the other drivers unlucky enough to be on the road during your commute, migraine throbbing in your head, overcome by the sheer dread of another eight-plus hours on the job? Do you stalk into your place of employment with mumbled greetings and a request not to be bothered before lunch?

Okay, so maybe it's unfair to use a person's morning attitude as a gauge of job satisfaction. But the point is still valid. If you wake up every morning dreading the day ahead, you may be in the wrong line of work. What's more, no amount of money is worth the misery of working a soul-deadening job.

WHAT ARE YOU ACCOMPLISHING?

Job descriptions can be misleading. If you want to boil things down to their basic elements, Michael Jordan's primary career responsibility was to throw an inflated ball through a metal rim. For that, he was paid over $30 million a year. The basic elements of his job description, however, do not take into account the entertainment and endorsement aspects of His Airness's career. They do not factor in his marketing appeal, the fact that his very presence at a game guaranteed hundreds of thousands of dollars in revenue for stadium and area merchants. They do not include the pleasure that his game brought to millions of basketball fans around the world.

To a (much) lesser degree, the same principle holds true for your job. On paper, your job description may involve little more than, say, troubleshooting computer software. Beyond that basic description, though, you should acknowledge that you keep the financial dealings of a multimillion dollar company running smoothly, thereby ensuring greater returns for the company's investors. Thinking globally, yet realistically, about your responsibilities is the key to determining what you're actually accomplishing.

Can you look beyond the everyday, mundane aspects of your job to see what you're accomplishing on a broader scale? If so, are you proud of what you're doing? Do you have a sense of accomplishment and satisfaction regarding your work? Are you affecting people's lives in a positive way? These are the intangibles that make a job worth doing.

WHAT IS GOD CALLING YOU TO DO?

God gave you natural talents, skills, and abilities for a reason. Are you putting those gifts to work in your job? If so, how? If not, should you be looking for another career? If you feel unfulfilled in your job, you may be able to trace your dissatisfaction to some untapped skills and abilities. We highly recommend that you stretch yourself as much as possible in your work to put as many of your talents and gifts to work as possible.

DON'T LIMIT YOUR OPTIONS

There's no reason to think you have to become a pastor or Sunday school teacher or missionary to be used by the Lord. God works through people in all walks of life to accomplish His will. All that's needed is a willing spirit.

The apostle Peter was a fisherman, and look what God did through him! Paul was tent maker. Luke was a doctor. Matthew was a tax collector, for crying out loud! Yet God used all of these people in ways they could not imagine. Who's to say he won't do the same through your career—whatever that career may be!

WOW!

Jobs You Won't Find on Any Résumé

If you ever decide to change careers, you'll find yourself in some pretty famous company. We all know Ronald Reagan was an actor before he became president. But you may be surprised at some of the former careers of other well-known people.

This Person . . .	Was Once a . . .
Dan Aykroyd	Postal worker
Sean Connery	Milkman
Elvis Costello	Computer programmer
Danny DeVito	Hairdresser
Whoopi Goldberg	Make-up artist for corpses
Adolf Hitler	Painter
Dustin Hoffman	Waiter
L. Ron Hubbard	Science fiction novelist
Steve Martin	Vendor at Disneyland
Geraldo Rivera	Lawyer
Sylvester Stallone	Gym teacher
Rod Stewart	Grave digger

WHAT'S HOT? WHAT'S NOT?
CAREER AND EMPLOYMENT PROJECTIONS
FOR THE TWENTY-FIRST CENTURY

What you'll find here are several lists of careers that are projected to be "hot" in the next millennium. Career and employment experts compile these lists to give college students and beginning job seekers an idea of which fields they might want to pursue. The reasoning is that if a field or industry is projected to grow throughout the next decade or two, it's good career choice.

We ask that you take this information with a grain of salt. Choosing a career based on how "hot" it will be in the future is like choosing a husband or wife based on life expectancy. Just because your mate's probably going to be around fifty years from now doesn't mean you're going to enjoy living with that person! Likewise, if you choose a job based solely on its future potential, you're asking for trouble. If it's not something that interests you now, it probably won't be something that interests you twenty years from now.

FASTEST GROWING INDUSTRIES

The *Career Guide to Industries*, published by the United States Bureau of Labor Statistics (yes, there's a bureau for labor statistics—your tax dollars hard at work), ranks careers from an industry perspective. The following industries are projected to grow faster than average between in the next decade.

Industry	Projected Rate of Growth
Computer and data processing services	95.7
Social services	93.1
Child care	73.0
Management and public relations	69.5
Motion picture production and distribution	60.8
Personnel supply services	56.6
Health services	43.4
Agriculture	40.5
Hotel and lodging	40.5
Amusement and recreation services	39.1
Air transportation	32.7
Eating and drinking places	33.0
Securities and commodities	29.9
Educational services	28.4
Advertising	27.5

WHAT IF YOU NEED TO LOOK FOR A JOB?

"Whatever you do, do it all for the glory of God" (1 Corinthians 10:31). This is the principle that guides all career matters for God's people. Whether you're a brain surgeon, a librarian, a systems analyst, or a photographer, you have a responsibility to use your career to bring glory to the Lord. But beyond this basic principle, the Bible has much to say about Christians and work.

PART OF THE PLAN

Our Heavenly Father happens to be a big fan of work. In fact, he created us with a natural capacity for it. Genesis 2:15 says God put Adam in the Garden of Eden "to work it and take care of it." God's plan for Adam holds true for us today. We were made to work.

Psalm 90:17 offers another incentive for labor. The verse suggests that work allows us to leave our mark on society. When a person's labor is blessed by the Lord, it becomes a lasting legacy, a testimony to the worker.

What's more, verses like Proverbs 10:4 and 14:23 equate hard work with wealth—if not material riches, then spiritual ones, the kind that really matter.

ALL WORK AND NO PLAY MAKES JACK . . . AN IDOLATER?

"You shall have no other gods before me" (Exodus 20:3).
"Keep yourselves from idols" (1 John 5:21).

To some people, these might seem like the easiest commandments in the Bible to obey. Let's face it: bowing down to a carved statue isn't real high on the list of modern temptations. But what if we defined *other gods* or *idols* as anything in our lives that is given higher priority than the Lord?

Hmmm. Let's talk about careers, shall we?

Careers matter in our society. Ever notice how often people allow themselves to be defined by what they do for a living?

- "My name's Sharon. I'm a sales rep for Carson Pirie Scott."
- "My mother will be happy when she hears I'm dating a doctor."
- "Now entering the studio are today's contestants: a high school science teacher from Akron, Ohio . . ."

Don't allow yourself to be defined by your career. And don't allow your career to become an idol. You may be surprised at how easily a job can dominate your life, if you allow it to. Keep in mind that your career is a means for glorifying God and fulfilling his will in your life. A career should be a priority in your life, but never your highest priority.

MILLENNIUM CAREER OVERVIEWS

SLOWEST GROWING INDUSTRIES

The Bureau of Labor Statistics' *Career Guide to Industries* also ranks the industries with the slowest projected growth rates. The following industries are projected to grow more slowly than average or decline in the next decade.

Industry	*Projected Rate of Growth*
Department stores	12.2
Public utilities	12.2
Radio and TV broadcasting	10.5
Banking	4.3
Aerospace manufacturing	2.5
Food processing	-0.4
Chemicals manufacturing (not drugs)	-4.0
Federal government	-5.2
Motor vehicle equipment manufacturing	-6.1
Mining and quarrying	-6.8
Steel manufacturing	-10.5
Oil and gas extraction	-14.3
Textile mill products manufacturing	-15.0
Electronics manufacturing	-16.3

FASTEST GROWING OCCUPATIONS

The busy little beavers at the Bureau of Labor Statistics also put out a list of the fastest growing careers from an *employee's* perspective. The following careers are projected to grow the most quickly in the next decade.

Career	Projected Rate of Growth
Home health aide	138%
Human service worker	136%
Personal/home care aide	130%
Computer engineer/scientist	112%
Systems analyst	110%
Physical/corrective therapy assistant/aide	93%
Physical therapist	88%
Paralegal	86%
Special education teacher	74%
Medical assistant	71%
Private detective	70%
Correction officer	70%
Child care worker	66%
Travel agent	66%
Radiologic technologist/technician	63%
Nursery worker	62%
Medical records technician	61%
Operations research analyst	61%
Occupational therapist	60%
Legal secretary	57%
Kindergarten/preschool teacher	54%

Career	*Projected Rate of Growth*
Manicurist	54%
Producer/director/actor/entertainer	54%
Speech pathologist/audiologist	51%
Flight attendant	51%
Guard	51%
Insurance adjuster/examiner/investigator	49%
Respiratory therapist	48%

YOU, YOUR CAREER, AND YOUR COMPUTER

Job Resources on the Internet

If you're searching for a job or job-related advice, man, are you ever living in the right age! With just a few keystrokes and click or two of the mouse, you have access to an almost unimaginable amount of help. The Internet may be a career-minded person's best friend. The key, of course, is knowing where to look in the vast reaches of cyberspace.

Ideally the best way to find the information you seek is through a long, involved exploration in which you simply follow links that seem interesting to you. However, if you don't have the time or patience for such an exploration, we've compiled a list of sites that may be of interest to you.

For your convenience, we've divided the sights into four categories: positions available (job listings), job search helps (advice for job seekers), salary information, and career advice.

Happy hunting!

POSITIONS AVAILABLE

Want to check the job market for dental assistants in the Scranton, Pennsylvania, area? Chances are you'll find a web site with that information.

Try these sites on for size:
America's Job Bank (http://www.ajb.dni.us/)
Career Mosaic (http://www.careermosaic.com)
Career Path (http://www.careerpath.com)
Career Resource Center (http://www.careers.org)
Career Web (http://www.careerweb.com/jobs)
CoolWorks (http://www.coolworks.com)
E-Span (http://www.espan.com)
Job Center (http://www.jobcenter.com)
Monster Board (http://www.monster.com)
Online Career Center (http://www.occ.org)

JOB SEARCH HELPS

How important are your references in your job search? How long should
you delay revealing your salary expectations in an interview? What should
you write in a follow-up letter? These questions and thousands like them
are answered online. If you have a question about your job search, you'll be
able to find an expert on the Internet who can answer it—free of charge.
Here are some sites to check out to find these experts.

Barron's (http://www.enews.com/magazines/barrons)
Business Week (http://www.enews.com/magazines/bw)
Economist (http://www.economist.com)
Forbes (http://www.forbes.com)
Inc. (http://www.enews.com/magazines/inc)
Journal of Commerce (http://www.enews.com/magazines/joc)
Los Angeles Times (http://www.latimes.com)
New York Times (http://www.nytimes.com)

U.S. Federal Government (http://www.lib.lsu.edu/gov/fedgov.html)
U.S. News and World Report (http://www.usnews.com)

SALARY INFORMATION

Want the latest numbers on how much your career is going to net you?
With just a few clicks of your mouse button, those figures and more will be
available to you. From aardvark trainer to zygote specialist, the Internet
runs the spectrum of career salaries. (Of course, the more obscure your
career choice, the harder you'll have to look for information. That means
you, aardvark trainers and zygote specialists.) Obviously we can't list all of
the sites dedicated to specific careers. Instead, we've selected sites that
provide more general databases.

Abbott, Langer & Associates (http://www.abbott-langer.com/)
The Bureau of Labor Statistics (http://stats.bls.gov/)
California State University of Northridge (http://www.csu.edu)
JobSmart (http://www.jobsmart)
JobWeb (http://jobweb.org)
The Riley Guide (http://www.dbm.com/jobguide)
Wageweb (http://www.wageweb.com/)
The Wall Street Journal Interactive Edition (http://careers.wsj.com/)

CAREER ADVICE

From tips on getting along with your boss to advice on dealing with sexual
harassment, you can find a lot of valuable career guidance in cyberspace-
provided, of course, that you know where to look. *We* know where to look,
and we've listed several sites that you should check out if you have a

question about or problem with your career.

America's CareerInfoNet (http://www.acinet.org/resource/careers)
Career Magazine (http://www.careermag.com)
Career Resource Center (http://www.careers.org)
Employer & Employee (http://www.employer-employee.com)
Entrepreneurial Edge (http://www.edgeonline.com)
The Job Resource (http://www.thejobresource.com/career/)
Job Show (http://www.jobshow.com)
The Mining Co. (http://careerplanning.miningco.com/)
Taunee Besson's Career Advice FAQs (http://www.cweb.com/bessonfaqs)
Vault Reports (http://www.vaultreports.com/career/career.shtml)

FUTURE FUNDS

HOW MUCH MONEY WILL YOU NEED FOR THE DAYS AHEAD?

Like it or not, if you're considering your future, sooner or later you're going to have to think about money. After all, the more money you make, the happier you'll be in the future, right?

Well, no.

In fact, if you structure your life around the goal of making as much money as possible, you can kiss your chances for a truly fulfilling future goodbye. Think we're exaggerating? Check out what God has to say about money in His Word:

- "Whoever loves money never has money enough; whoever loves wealth is never satisfied with his income." (Ecclesiastes 5:10)

- "No one can serve two masters. Either he will hate the one and love the other, or he will be devoted to the one and despise the other. You cannot serve both God and Money." (Matthew 6:24)

- "For the love of money is a root of all kinds of evil. Some people, eager for money, have wandered from the faith and pierced themselves with many griefs." (1 Timothy 6:10)

Earning money isn't evil. Worrying about having enough money later in life isn't a sin. But making money the number one priority in your life is wrong—and it leads to all kinds of trouble.

Don't let dollar signs cloud your vision. Remember, money is just one of many factors to consider when planning your future.

BEYOND THE GREEN

For a truly fulfilling life, there are factors other than money that you should weigh. Here are some questions you should ask yourself as you plan for your future:

- Am I effectively using my God-given gifts and abilities?
- Am I proud of the work I do, both in and out of the office?
- Am I sufficiently challenged intellectually?
- Have I surrounded myself with potential mentors and advisors?
- Have I established a God-honoring environment in my home?
- Am I fulfilling my responsibilities to my community?

If you are considering a career move based primarily on your felt need to earn more money for your future, here are some questions that you should consider:

- Will you be working with people you respect and get along with?
- Does your boss's personality suit yours?

- Does the company produce quality products or service?
- Does it have a good reputation in the industry?
- Is it committed to improvement?
- Does it offer health insurance or continuing-education assistance?
- Is there anything about the company's practices that disturbs you?
- Does the company promote from within?
- Does it encourage professional growth?

MAKING ENDS MEET

Before you start examining your financial intake needs, you should probably take a hard look at what your monthly output will

WOW!

Great Quotes on Money

"**Money never made a man happy yet, nor will it. There is nothing in its nature to produce happiness. The more a man has, the more he wants. That was a true proverb of the wise man, rely upon it: 'Better is little with the fear of the Lord, than great treasure, and trouble therewith.' "**
—**Benjamin Franklin**

"**Make all you can, save all you can, give all you can."** —**John Wesley**

"**The making of money is necessary for daily living, but money-making is apt to degenerate into money-loving, and then the deceitfulness of riches enters in and spoils our spiritual life."**
—**Billy Graham**

be. How much will it cost you to maintain at least a decent standard of living? What bills do you need to factor into your budget? In other words, what's the minimum amount you need in order to live?

Below we've listed several possible monthly expenditures for you to consider. Only when you've taken all of them into account can you start thinking about your future financial requirements.

- Tithing (What percentage of your income do you give back to the Lord?)
- Mortgage (Is refinancing an option? Can you lower your monthly payments at all?)
- Utilities (How much do you pay for electricity, gas, and water? How high are your phone bills? Do you need cable TV?)
- Food (Do you watch your grocery bills closely? Do you eat out most of the time?)
- Car (Are you making payments on your vehicle?)
- Maintenance (How much money do you need to put away each month in order to cover tune-ups, oil changes, and unexpected repairs?)

CATCH A CLUE

Need Money Help?

There are many good Christian books and ministries that can help you with your finances. There are also free resources available on the web. Consider trying the following:
http://www.crown.org
http://www.crosswalk.com
http://www.good-steward.org
http://www.ronblue.com
http://www.soundmindinvesting.com
http://www.quicken99.com
http://www.cheapskatesmonthly.com
http://www.nodebtnews.com
http://www.cfcministry.org
http://www.gpgonline.com
http://www.debtfreeconcepts.com
http://www.finacenter.com
http://www.idg.net
http://www.mastering-finances.com

- Commute (If you drive to work, how much do you pay for gas? If you take public transportation, how much do you pay for bus or train tickets?)
- Insurance (How much do you pay for auto insurance? Do you have life insurance payments to consider?)
- Loans (Do you—or your kids—have school bills to consider?)
- Credit cards (What bills do you have to pay off?)

- Wardrobe (Does your job require you to regularly purchase expensive clothing?)
- Spending cash (How often do you buy CDs, rent movies, play golf, or attend concerts? How much money do you spend each month on hobbies?)

Total up the numbers for each category. The sum you arrive at is the absolute minimum you'll need in order to survive each month. When you're considering your financial future, this is the figure you should start with. You can make changes to this figure by cutting back in certain areas or by adding things that we've left out. The point is, you need to have a base number to work with in order to know what you need in the future.

HIGH PRESSURE PERFORMANCE

A NEW, STRESSFUL WORLD

Stress kills. The word may not show up on any coroner's report or death certificate, but it kills just the same. Everything from heart attacks to suicides have been blamed on stress. While it may be difficult to avoid stress altogether, there are plenty of things you can do to lessen its effect on your life.

Do what you can to address it at work.
You may be surprised to find out that the biggest contributor to your stressful lifestyle is you—or more specifically—your work habits. With some key changes in the way you go about your job, you could reduce your stress load by 50 percent or more.

The first area you'll want to look at is time management. Is your stress the product of a never-ending game of "Beat the Clock"? Are you constantly feeling the pressure of deadlines and commitments? The simple solution is to guard against scheduling—or allowing others to schedule—more activities every day than you can possibly finish. Okay, maybe it's not a simple solution, but it's a solution. A manageable workload is the key to mental health. That's not to say that you can rid yourself of tight schedules completely. There will be times when long hours and quick work are absolutely necessary. But those times should be the exception, not the rule

Of course not all time management problems are created by outside sources like deadlines and impatient bosses. Some are the result of procrastination. If you're the type of person who prefers to put things off until the last minute, you're just asking for a juicy mouthful of stress. Practice good time management skills by tackling projects as soon as you get them. Resist the tendency to flirt with deadlines. Get your work done early whenever possible.

Finally, you may need to learn to delegate responsibilities to help you reduce your workload and stress level. If you have qualified people ready, willing, and able to help you with a project, it's foolish to try to do it on your own. Take advantage of all the resources available to you.

Seek help from your family and friends.

You may think it's noble to suffer alone and not trouble your friends and family members with your stress problems. Well, it's not noble, and you're not fooling anyone. Anybody who knows you well will recognize when you're stressed out. And they'll want to help. Denying the problem or sweeping it under a rug will only serve to distance you from the ones who care most about you.

Let your friends and family help you. Share with them what you're going through and how you're feeling. You don't have to monopolize every conversation with your misery, but also don't pull any punches. Be honest with them. Not only will they be able to give you emotional support, they may also find practical ways for relieving your stress in other areas—by keeping household affairs in order, for example. The point is, do not ignore your God-given support system by trying to shield your family and friends from the pressure you're under.

DEVELOP A STRESS-RELIEVING HOBBY

One New York stockbroker relieves his stress by flying fighter jets over the Arizona desert. An Oregon credit officer bungee jumps off 180-foot bridges. A Colorado financial analyst practices feng shui, the ancient Chinese art of ordering one's environment to live in total harmony. A Minnesota accountant performs in jazz clubs. All of these people have

Take a break

Science fiction author Arthur C. Clarke proposed, in a 1973 interview, that mankind declare "the whole of 2000 a holiday. If we make it to there, we'll be fully justified."

found stress reduction in their hobbies. They claim that the focus their hobbies require allows them to forget about the pressures of the business world, even if it's for a short time.

You'll notice that "stress-relieving" and "relaxing" are not necessarily the same thing. A hobby that provides an adrenaline rush or physical exertion can be just as effective in relieving stress as needlepoint or reading. In other words, if you can find a hobby that reduces your stress by taking your mind off the pressures of work, go for it.

TAKE IT TO THE LORD

Do not neglect your time with the Lord. Maintain a regular prayer time as well as a regular Bible study, perhaps with a group of trusted friends. If you're not currently in one, a weekly Bible study/prayer group can do wonders for your stress. Being able to share with other believers exactly what you're going through can be quite therapeutic. Ask the Lord to help you relieve the harmful stress in your life. Similarly, ask Him to help you find ways to reduce the amount of pressure you face every day.

SECTION 9
YOUR OWN SPIRITUAL HEALTH

A WORLD OF DISTRACTIONS

The history of God's people reveals, among other things, that we are forgetful, easily distracted people. "Prone to wander, Lord, I feel it; prone to leave the God I love" is the way the old hymn puts it. It's not difficult to see why this is true. With worldly enticements and devilish temptations from *without*, and fleshly desires churning *within*, it's a huge battle to stay focused on God and to keep walking with Him.

In recognition of this human frailty, the Bible says much about remembering (Note: The word *remember* is found 166x in the NIV Bible, along with numerous admonitions to *not forget* God!). Old Testament saints made it a common practice to bring to mind God's great acts in their festivals and psalms. They often erected monuments to commemorate divine encounters and deliverances. In the New Testament we find similar customs, the most obvious being Christ's institution of the Lord's Supper. This simple meal of wine and bread was intended by Jesus to be celebrated regularly so that believers would be reminded often of Christ (His sacrifice, His presence, His coming again).

GREAT BIBLE PASSAGES ABOUT FOCUSING ON GOD

"When you have eaten and are satisfied, praise the LORD your God for the good land he has given you. Be careful that you do not forget the LORD your God, failing to observe his commands, his laws and his decrees that I am giving you this day. Otherwise, when you eat and are satisfied, when you build fine houses and settle down, and when your herds and flocks grow large and your silver and gold increase and all you have is multiplied, then your heart will become proud and you will forget the LORD your God." (Deuteronomy 8:10-14)

"But seek first his kingdom and his righteousness, and all these things will be given to you as well." (Matthew 6:33)

 "Let us fix our eyes on Jesus, the author and perfecter of our faith." (Hebrews 12:2)

 "Set your minds on things above, not on earthly things." (Colossians 3:2)

"What is more, I consider everything a loss compared to the surpassing greatness of knowing Christ Jesus my Lord, for whose sake I have lost all things. I consider them rubbish, that I may gain Christ." (Philippians 3:8)

"So we fix our eyes not on what is seen, but on what is unseen. For what is seen is temporary, but what is unseen is eternal." (2 Corinthians 4:18)

"By faith Moses, when he had grown up, refused to be known as the son of Pharaoh's daughter. He chose to be mistreated along with the people of God rather than to enjoy the pleasures of sin for a short time. He regarded disgrace for the sake of Christ as of greater value than the treasures of Egypt, because he was looking ahead to his reward. By faith he left Egypt, not fearing the king's anger; he persevered because he saw him who is invisible" (Hebrews 11:24–27)

RESOURCES THAT CAN HELP US STAY FOCUSED ON GOD

Christian Friends
Ecclesiastes 4:9-10 says:

> "Two are better than one, because they have a good return for their work: If one falls down, his friend can help him up. But pity the man who falls and has no one to help him up!"

How true this is! We all need a person or two in our lives who knows us, loves us, and, most importantly, shares our desire to walk with God.

Church
Faithful church involvement (not just sporadic attendance) can be a tremendous help to us spiritually.

Personal Disciplines
It's a great thing to be surrounded by other believers who are challenging you spiritually and helping keep you focused. It's *not* a good thing to depend *entirely* upon such external resources for your spiritual health. You also need to be developing an internal spiritual focus that will keep you on target during those times in life when you're not surrounded by Christian influences.

The single best way to develop a godward mindset and focus is to begin the practice of spending time with God every day. Whether you call this practice having devotions, a quiet time, or a daily appointment with God, the idea is to get alone with the Lord and spend time talking to and listening to Him. It's during this time that you shove worldly distractions and trivial concerns from your mind, and bring to mind the things that are true—about God, about you, about the world, about the purpose of life.

The Christians who are persistent in doing this are far more likely to stay focused on God. The believers who neglect this practice (and depend solely on an occasional sermon or Christian gathering to keep them strong) are the ones who are likely to drift away from God.

Scripture Memory & Meditation

The psalmist wrote,

> "I have hidden your word in my heart that I might not sin against you" (Psalm 119:11).

Here's the bottom-line of what that verse means: When we store God's truth (i.e. His Word) in our hearts and minds, and when we make it our practice to meditate upon that truth, we stay on track spiritually.

Meditation is not some passive Eastern practice where we sit cross-legged and hum quietly. It's an active process of bringing scriptural truth to mind, thinking hard about it, and examining it from every angle. The more we ponder, reflect, cogitate on the Word, the more chance it has to seep into our souls. Over time, these biblical truths move from being "nice ideas" to "bedrock convictions." Our attitudes change. Our values are shaped into the very values of God.

HOW TO GROW SPIRITUALLY (BIBLE STUDY, PRAYER)
QUIZ O' THE DAY!

Fact: The New Testament indicates that our outer actions are a good measure of our inner spiritual health (Matthew 7:16-20).

Question: What could we conclude about someone who
- Watches only religious movies like *The Ten Commandments*
- Memorizes the Gospel of Matthew (in Greek)
- Reads the complete works of C. S. Lewis annually
- Shares the *Four Spiritual Laws* with strangers in airports
- Preaches with a bullhorn at downtown bus stops
- Fasts during the Thanksgiving break
- Goes to all three Sunday services so he can take communion three times
- Gives her entire paycheck to missionaries in Malawi
- Throws his TV out the window and pledges to read only the Bible
- Spends vacations and breaks working at an inner city soup question?

Answer: Nothing! External actions alone do not necessarily indicate spiritual life, health, or growth. (If you don't believe it, just consider the Pharisees in the Gospels.)

SPIRITUAL LIFE AND SPIRITUAL GROWTH

In the physical realm, from the moment we are born we begin a long process of physical growth. We learn to crawl, climb, splash around in the toilet (yeehaw!), walk, talk, take care of ourselves (at least theoretically), etc. Such growth is normal, natural, and expected. A failure to develop in this manner is an indication of sickness and/or retardation (picture a college freshman in diapers and sucking a pacifier!).

It's important to realize that a similar process is also at work in the spiritual realm. We are "born again" (John 3) when we put our faith in Christ. As new believers we

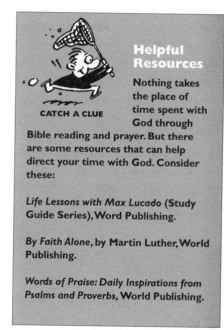

CATCH A CLUE

Helpful Resources

Nothing takes the place of time spent with God through Bible reading and prayer. But there are some resources that can help direct your time with God. Consider these:

Life Lessons with Max Lucado **(Study Guide Series), Word Publishing.**

By Faith Alone, **by Martin Luther, World Publishing.**

Words of Praise: Daily Inspirations from Psalms and Proverbs, **Word Publishing.**

are, in a very real sense, spiritual infants who need to grow up. When we do *not* grow spiritually, something is deeply wrong.

THE COMPONENTS OF GROWTH

Physical growth requires proper nutrition plus exercise plus time. Guess what? It's the same in the spiritual realm. Growing spiritually requires a healthy intake of God's Word (hearing it taught, reading it, studying it, memorizing it, meditating upon it), and a commitment to exercise our faith daily through prayer, service, witnessing, etc. Spiritual growth takes time. We'll have some "growth spurts" (just as we do in the physical realm) where we seem to take big leaps forward. But by and large, our spiritual growth will be slow and almost imperceptible.

MOTIVES FOR GROWTH

Some Christians fall into a kind of selfish pride when it comes to spiritual growth. More than wanting to grow so that they can know God better, glorify Him more fully, and serve Him more effectively, they actually want to grow so they can impress other people. For these few, the real goal is to be perceived as "godly." This explains their zeal for Scripture memory or deep Bible study. Sometimes a secret competition can even develop between believers as they vie for the title of "most spiritually mature." Check your own motives for wanting to grow. Are you just eager to be and do what God wants, or is there a hidden agenda in your heart?

OBSTACLES TO GROWTH

Some believers are spiritually malnourished. They erroneously think they can get by on a minimum of true spiritual food. Guess what? A sermon here, a few verses there, or a Bible promise every once in a while won't cut it. That's a kind of "spiritual anorexia"! No one can thrive living like that.

Still other believers settle for "processed and packaged" spiritual food. That is they opt for a diet of Christian books and magazine articles. While such materials aren't necessarily *bad*, they can never measure up to the "100% (super)natural" goodness of the pure Word of God. It's like the difference in bland, canned corn that has been stripped of most of its vitamins and that you end up putting artificial margarine on, and fresh, right-off-the-stalk corn-on-the-cob that you slather real butter on . . . SO sweet, and crunchy, and fresh . . .

The point? If you're spending more time reading books *about the Bible*, than you are actually reading *the Bible itself*, you'll never grow as much or as fast as you otherwise could.

SECTION 10
YOUR FAMILY AND THE MILLENNIUM

GROW A FAMILY TREE

The new millennium will keep you busy. The busier you become, the more likely you are to put aside some things that should come first: like time with your family.

There are some good ways to use technology and the changes to do things *together.* No matter your children's age, find some hobbies you can do together. One hobby is quickly becoming popular and becoming easier to do: Genealogy research.

By starting with your parents and extended family, you should be able to quickly begin your tree and stretch it back to the early 1900's (or earlier!).

CATCH A CLUE

Places to Look

Genealogy work is becoming easier than ever thanks to the Internet. You can download free genealogy programs. For examples:

http://www.danmorin.com/ generations/
This program is harder to use than some, but it is free.

http://www.gendesigner.com
This program must be purchased after a thirty day trial period expires.

You can also find sites dedicated to genealogy. The Mormon Church, famous for their genealogy work, has begun putting their database on the Internet. Visit their site at http:// www.familysearch.org and see if you can find your family!

FOR A FUTURE TIME

TIME CAPSULE

Create a time capsule that will be opened by someone in your family one hundred years from now.

Work together as a family to consider what might go inside. Find a sturdy crate and pass along a piece of history to the next generation.

Ideas to Consider:

- print out a copy of your favorite web page.
- Write a letter telling future generations what your favorite technology is, your favorite music or movie. Tell them what you think life will be like 100 years from now.
- a picture of your family
- coins from the current year
- Sunday's paper
- current magazines, TV guides, and catalogues
- grocery receipt (to show prices of key indicators: bread, milk, soda, candy bar, etc.
- a church bulletin

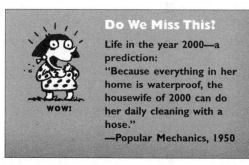

WOW!

Do We Miss This?

Life in the year 2000—a prediction:
"Because everything in her home is waterproof, the housewife of 2000 can do her daily cleaning with a hose."
—Popular Mechanics, 1950

EDU-TAIN TOGETHER

THE FAMILY THAT LEARNS TOGETHER . . .

One of the marks of our time is that everyone is trying to make learning *fun*. Find ways to have fun while learning together.

This is often a challenge for parents and their kids because their interests are often quite different. The interests you have developed were probably influenced by world you grew up in. Your children's interests will be shaped by their world.

Find common ground. It might not be easy, but keep looking.

SACRIFICE, IF YOU NEED TO

No matter how hard you try, you might not find common ground. You might feel like you're from two different planets. If so, sacrifice. You might not have the same interests, but choose to learn about your children's interests anyway. It may be uninteresting to you or confusing, but try anyway. Your effort may be difficult, but it will go along way.

TEACH YOUR KIDS TO DISCERN

Technology isn't evil. But people can use technology for evil. Teach your children the difference. Show them how to use exciting new technologies in good ways. In doing so, you'll pass on your values and help them make good decisions. And that's a legacy they'll leave the twenty-*second* century.

CATCH A CLUE

The Family that Surfs Together . . .

When most people think of surfing the 'net, they think that it's like an individual sport (like swimming or running.) You usually do it alone.

One way to interact together is to surf together. Explore your common interests sitting side-by-side (but no fighting over the mouse!).

If you have children, start at Berit's Best Sites for Children (http://db.cochran.com/li_toc:theoPage.db). This site reviews good, safe sites for children. It reviews educational sites, as well as games, kids' home pages, and other fun pages. Here a few highlights from that site:

http://www.funschool.com
Funschool has lots of great educational games and activities. There are areas for preschool, kindergarten, first grade, second grade, and third grade. Topics include math and reading, concentration, spot-the difference, coloring, the environment, seasons, animals, food groups, and more.

http://www.kidscarnival.com/
This site has learning games, puzzles, mazes and activities dealing with colors, shapes, time, numbers letters, and more. The stories included are brief and don't have illustrations.

http://animabets.com/
Lots of learning activities, puzzles and games featuring a cast of animal characters. Created for children aged 5 to 10.

http://www.knowble.com/
Learn a bit about ballet, space, airplanes, seaports, and other topics. There are also arcade and adventure games, paper planes to make, pictures to color, dot-to-dot pages, and more. The site is hosted by the Knowbles cartoon characters and features lots of animations and sounds.

http://www.stickerworld.org/
This is a unique site where you can create web pages, trade electronic stickers, play games, take quizzes, create Sticker Lib stories, and communicate in a private and safe community. This site is monitored regularly to ensure appropriate content. For children aged 6 - 12. From the Children's Television Workshop Online.

http://www.haringkids.com/
Haring Kids features simple books, art activities and games intended to inspire a love of learning and art in children. Teachers will find numerous lesson plans for language arts, visual and performing arts, math, and so on. You need to use the animated menu on the left side of the window to get around this site. For early elementary kids and teachers. Uses Shockwave Flash.

http://www.shoozoo.com/
At ShooZoo, unusual animal characters live in shoes. You can play Shockwave games, such as Feed the Froggie, a concentration game and jigsaw puzzle. Print, assemble and color your own storybook and write a story to go along with the pictures. There are also coloring pages to print and a gallery of kids' pictures. For ages 3 to 10.

http://www.magickeys.com/books/count/index.html
This simple counting book is illustrated with animated pink bunnies. On each number page they do different tricks. Fun for children learning to count.

http://www.aplusmath.com/
Play games like bingo, discover hidden pictures, test yourself with flashcards and use the homework helper that will tell if your answers are correct. For elementary age children.

INDEX

INDEX

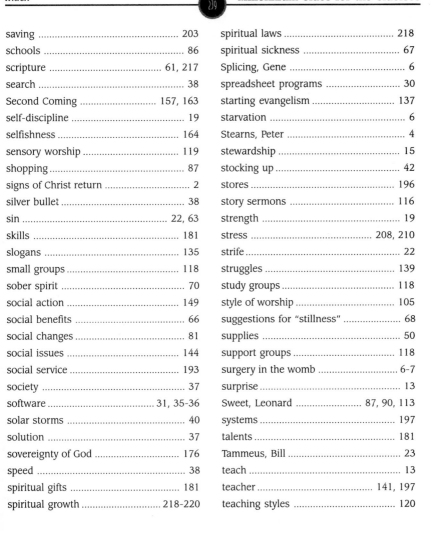